RIGHT TO CARRY

I Carry a Gun
A Cop Is Too Heavy!

Alan Gottlieb

&

Dave Workman

Introduction by Tim Schmidt
President of United States Concealed Carry Association

Merril Press
Bellevue, WA 98005

RIGHT TO CARRY

is published by
Merril Press, P.O. Box 1682, Bellevue, WA 98009.
www.merrilpress.com
Phone: 425-454-7009
Distributed to the book trade by
Midpoint Trade Books, 27 W. 20th Street, New York, N.Y. 10011
www.midpointtradebooks.com
Phone: 212-727-0190

FIRST EDITION

LIBRARY OF CONGRESS CATALOGING-IN-PUBLICATION DATA

Print ISBN 0-936783-68-0

PRINTED IN THE UNITED STATES OF AMERICA

RIGHT TO CARRY

DEDICATION

To the hundreds of thousands of law-abiding citizens who have used firearms to defend themselves and their loved ones, and the thousands of instructors who taught them, and to The Founders, who understood that the right to Bear arms is the right to Carry them.

CONTENTS

FOREWARD

Few people in the firearms community have the long and proven history that Alan Gottlieb does. When he founded the Second Amendment Foundation (SAF) and the Citizens Committee for the Right to Keep and Bear Arms (CCRKBA) over 40 years ago, I'm not sure he had any idea just how influential—and vital—his humble non-profit corporation and its lobbying affiliate—now over 650,000 members strong—would become in both honoring and defending their namesake right.

The way I see it, you don't spend the better part of your entire life fighting for something you don't passionately believe in, and I can't think of anyone more loyal to the Second Amendment and all it stands for than Alan Gottlieb. In fact, it's that exact trait—that loyalty—that gives an off-the-charts brilliant man like Alan a real sense of authenticity. It's also one of the main reasons I like, admire, and trust him so much.

Now, I have to admit: I was a bit taken aback, albeit honored, when Alan thought to ask me to share a few words to introduce his and Dave Workman's latest work, Right to Carry. It's always an unexpected—and humbling—experience when someone you both respect and look up to asks for your help—or your perspective—on something you've deemed to be of the utmost importance.

I'll never forget, for instance, how I felt the first time my dad—my oldest and most influential mentor and the man who imparted to me his infamous "if it is to be, it's up to me" wisdom—sought out my advice and expertise on a critical business project.

I suppose it's not all that different than the feeling I still get knowing that hundreds of thousands of responsibly armed Americans all across the country are invested enough in the work I do through the United States Concealed Carry Association (USCCA) that they continue to ask me questions about everything from where I choose to carry my firearm to how I train to best protect the ones I love.

It's certainly how I felt when Alan and Dave, men who's spent over four decades defending the Second Amendment and fighting for people like you and me, thought that I might have something worthwhile to say about the right to carry a gun for self-defense.

Of course, I do have some thoughts on the matter, but I think a little context is in order first.

My grand debut into the world of firearms—or at least the idea of owning and carrying a firearm for self-defense—took place at about 35,000 feet above sea level. See, it was on an airplane, almost 20 years ago now, that I first encountered Robert Boatman's "The Constitutional Right and Social Obligation to Carry a Gun"—an article that awoke my inner patriot and—quite honestly—changed my entire life.

See, that article forced me, as a brand new father, to ask myself an incredibly important, powerful, and potentially life-changing question: Am I willing—and am I ready—to do absolutely everything in my power to keep my family safe? (I knew I was willing...but I wasn't so sure I was "ready"—at least not in the practical sense of carrying a firearm every day.)

I had this tiny new baby who was now dependent on me for absolutely everything. (If you're a parent, you know what I'm talking about.) It was exciting, sure, but it was also incredibly scary. I can still remember how it felt when my wife Tonnie and I brought Tim Jr. home for the first time. I can clearly recall thinking about this innocent new life and how I was now responsible for providing him with everything he needed. I was responsible for keeping him safe. And it just ignited something in me that I had never felt before. (I guess that's why Robert Boatman's article hit me so hard on that airplane.)

I knew I had to do something. As it turns out, that "something" meant learning anything and everything I could about firearms and self-defense.

But I ran into a huge roadblock: there simply wasn't enough information out there to help me get started. Although there were people like Alan Gottlieb and Dave Workman already working feverishly to defend the Second Amendment, there weren't any books or magazines dedicated specifically to the concealed carry lifestyle, and there were no resources available to help me feel confident in protecting myself and my family with a gun.

And so I did what any "sane" person would have done: I decided to create what I felt was missing. As it turns out, that little article on the airplane is where Concealed Carry Magazine first found its roots. And the guiding principles in that article provided the foundation on which I built the United States Concealed Carry Association—an organization dedicated to educating and training responsible American gun owners and providing powerful legal and financial protection if they're ever forced to defend themselves.

And so now you're starting to see how it all ties together:

The Right To Carry is directly related to my own personal firearms and concealed carry journey. And perhaps it will help carve out a path for you, too.

See, it takes a special person to own and carry a firearm for self-defense. These individuals—"responsibly armed Americans," as I've grown fond of calling them—understand the fragility and value the innocence of human life. In fact, they value it so much that they're overwhelmed by the desire (and responsibility) to protect and defend that innocent life at all costs. It's what drives them in all they do. It's why they train. It's why they carry their guns every day. And it's why they continue to fight for the freedom to exercise their Second Amendment rights.

And as important as it is for these responsible, law-abiding Americans to stand up as individuals, there's value—and strength—in numbers. I believe that we are more powerful together.

That's also why pro-gun organizations like the Second Amendment Foundation (SAF), who is, according to their mission statement, "dedicated to promoting a better understanding about our Constitutional heritage to privately own and possess firearms," are so incredibly important.

That's why Alan Gottlieb and Dave Workman—who have written and co-written over 20 books, most of which are directly related to guns and gun rights—are such important people to have on our side. What they manage to convey in Right to Carry is what you've come to expect from someone who understands what's at stake: that just because we have the right to carry a firearm for self-defense doesn't eliminate the responsibility that comes with it. As Alan and Dave poignantly explain in the final chapter:

"Responsibility. It comes with every civil right whether some of us like that or not, and those who abuse their exercise of any right with boorish behavior do no credit to the right, or to anyone else who exercises it."

They continue: "No civil right is unlimited. 'Shall not be infringed' does not mean people can be careless or negligent with firearms and get a pass. While Americans enjoy the right to keep and bear arms, this right is not there to be abused. The first word in this chapter was responsibility. It should be considered the first and last word in gun ownership."

To keep and bear arms is an inalienable, God-given right—one affirmed by the U.S. Constitution and exercised by millions of Americans all across our great nation. But we must treat that right with the great care and respect it deserves.

It's comforting to know that as more and more Americans are making the choice to protect their families with guns, there are also people who continue to stand up and fight for the right to keep and bear arms—people who do everything in their power to preserve the freedoms we hold so dear. And in my humble opinion, no one does that better than Alan Gottlieb and Dave Workman.

Tim Schmidt
President and Founder
USCCA

1: THE PUBLIC IS PACKING

"A well regulated Militia, being necessary to the security of a free State, the right of the people to keep and bear Arms, shall not be infringed."—II *Amendment*

Amid the apparently never-ending debate over the Second Amendment – a discussion steeped in emotion and denial from gun prohibitionists who, after having lost the argument over whether the amendment protects and affirms an individual civil right or a so-called "collective right" of states to form and maintain militias have stubbornly acknowledged that the right is an individual one – a new front in the battle over firearm civil rights has emerged.

This battle took on a new urgency and complexion in the aftermath of the terrorist attack in San Bernardino. If radical Islamists could strike in a community like that, they could launch an attack anywhere, the people reasoned. That bloody rampage ignited a spike in gun sales and applications for concealed carry licenses and permits, and even people who had never before even considered *owning* a gun were suddenly compelled to not only head to gun shops, they now also wanted to *carry* defensive firearms.

We have advanced a few rungs up the civil rights ladder beyond the point where most, but hardly all, gun control advocates begrudgingly agree people have a right to keep a gun in the home. However, the most extreme anti-gun groups, such as the Michael Bloomberg-backed Moms Demand Action for Gun Sense in America, continue to abhor the notion that law-abiding citizens can actually *bear* arms; that is, to carry a defensive firearm on one's person outside the home or place of business, for personal protection.

It is a sometimes nasty and invariably dramatic battle oft played to the cameras with all the self-righteous concern of an Academy Award-worthy performance.

The question of whether this right can be regulated is being booted around the various federal courts like a political football. The U.S. Supreme Court has at least three times turned down an opportunity to consider a case that might put this question to rest. Gun control extremists have attempted all manner of strategies to marginalize and socially blackball legally armed citizens – occasionally with the unintentional assistance of those same citizens, whom we will discuss at greater length in Chapter Twelve – but they have encountered one major obstacle: Public sentiment.

A growing segment of the population wants to be armed. By some estimates, as many as 11 to 12 million-plus citizens are licensed to carry across the United States. For example, since Illinois lawmakers adopted a concealed carry statute in 2013 following successful federal lawsuits filed independently by the Second Amendment Foundation (*Moore v. Madigan*) and National Rifle Association (*Shepard v. Madigan*), tens of thousands of Prairie State residents have obtained carry permits, continuing a pattern that has followed passage of similar laws in most other states over the past 20 years.

As the late Supreme Court Justice Antonin Scalia wrote in his majority opinion in *District of Columbia v.*

Dick Anthony Heller which struck down the handgun ban in Washington, D.C. in June 2008, "Whatever the reason, handguns are the most popular weapon chosen by Americans for self-defense in the home, and a complete prohibition of their use is invalid."

Despite claims by gun control organizations that gun ownership is dwindling, the National Shooting Sports Foundation (NSSF) noted that, for 2014 – the most recent year for which data was available – the total economic impact of the firearms industry was $42.9 *billion*, a 125-percent increase since 2008, when the economy received a $19.1 *billion* benefit from the sale of firearms and ammunition.

That is significant for a reason people might overlook. When the Supreme Court handed down its first landmark ruling on the Second Amendment in the *Heller* case, it turned the gun control movement on its ear. That was the ruling that recognized the right to keep and bear arms is a fundamental individual civil right, *protected* by, not merely *granted* by, the Second Amendment.

Two years later, in June 2010, the high court again issued a Second Amendment ruling in *McDonald v. City of Chicago* – A second Amendment Foundation case – that incorporated that ruling to the states. That is, the individual right to keep and bear arms not only placed a limit on the federal government, but also on state and local governments. While it seems clear that some appointed-for-life federal court judges still decline to see it that way, and hand down opinions reflective of this state-of-denial, it remains that the citizens have this right, and increasing numbers of them are exercising it.

According to the NSSF, the firearms industry today provides more than 263,000 full-time equivalent jobs, a 58 percent growth in employment for that industry from 2008.

This steady increase in firearms and ammunition business also coincides with the election of Barack Obama as president. A proponent of gun control since his days as an Illinois state senator, Mr. Obama acknowledged during an interview with ABC News that he was disappointed that he hadn't been able to push more gun control during his time in office. But, he also said that he was not giving up that fight.

One thing that gun control proponents have never quite figured out about American citizens is that when they are told there might be some restrictions placed on certain things, and most notably firearms, people head for the nearest gun shop or gun show. Mention an ammunition shortage, and these same people will line up at sporting goods stores to buy the shelves clean. Tell them they might face increased regulations on gun ownership or the ability to carry a firearm, they will submit concealed carry applications by the bushel.

As reported by Breitbart.com, gun sales "soared" in 2013 with more than 21 million background checks conducted by the FBI for firearms purchases that year. This was a new record, and it did not cover all the guns sold or traded that year, as private transactions in most states do not require such invasive checks.

Perhaps not surprisingly to Second Amendment activists, during the same period that gun sales spiked, violent crime declined. This is a hotly contested subject, as gun control proponents have offered their own studies that suggest violent crime is highest where gun ownership, and especially concealed carry, has climbed in recent years.

But according to Breitbart, "These record gun sales and the subsequent reduction in crime square perfectly with a Congressional Research Service report covered by Breitbart News on December 4, 2013. That study showed that the number of privately owned firearms in America increased from 192 million in 1994 to 310 million in 2009. At the same time, 'firearm-related murder and non-negligent homicide' fell from 6.6 per 100,000 Americans in 1993 to 3.6 per 100,000 in 2000."

"The bottom line," according to the story, "more guns equals less crime."

Not so fast, say gun control proponents who insist otherwise. In a report headlined "The Impact of Right to Carry Laws and the NRC Report: The Latest Lessons for the Empirical Evaluation of Law and Policy," published in 2014 by Stanford law professor John J. Donohue III, Stanford law student Abhay Aneja and Johns Hopkins doctoral student Alexandria Zhang, they suggested that Right-to-carry laws may contribute to increased violence. The Huffington Post noted at the time that, "Among violent crimes, the most significant increase came in aggravated assault, which may have risen by nearly 33 percent, according to the report. The researchers also found that from 1999 to 2010, murder rates rose in eight states that adopted right-to-carry laws."

The Huffington Post also quoted Daniel Webster, director of the Johns Hopkins Center for Gun Policy and Research, who explained that the report "corrected a number of flaws in the data" through the use of "new statistical methods." Webster maintained that right-to-carry laws "increase firearms-related assaults" but he acknowledged that "the exact magnitude of that effect is uncertain."

Likewise, Stanford University reported that the Donohue-Zhang-Aneja study "confirms that right-to-carry gun laws are linked to an increase in violent crime." The Stanford release quoted Donohue in an interview, noting that he is a C. Wendell and Edith M. Carlsmith Professor of Law.

Donohue told the publication that research based on data available prior to 1992 had indicated that such laws are followed by a decrease in violent crime. However, the National Research Council released a report in 2004 that, by extending the available data through 2000 "revealed no credible statistical evidence these particular laws reduced crime."

What is really going on here? Perhaps another quote from Prof. Donohue in the Stanford article sums it up: "Different statistical models can yield different estimated effects, and our ability to ascertain the best model is imperfect." Translation: We're not entirely certain. But, of course, that seems to be the nature of a lot of research projects. Such reports "suggest" conclusions but never really seem to arrive at one, therefore justifying more research, sort of a perpetual guaranteed employment program.

Here's another Donohue quote from the same article: "The totality of the evidence based on educated judgments about the best statistical models suggests that right-to-carry laws are associated with substantially higher rates" of aggravated assault, rape, robbery and murder.

It's not that researchers are trying to be evasive. It's just that it seems many of them simply do not care to paint themselves into a corner, which makes sense.

And Donohue was absolutely right when he noted that different statistical models can yield different estimated effects.

It's what happens to the suggestions and the data produced by Donohue and others that is of concern. Now is a good time to recall what Samuel Clemmons, aka Mark Twain, said: "There are lies, damned lies and statistics," a quote he reportedly attributed to Benjamin Disraeli, but apparently doesn't show up in any of Disraeli's writings. Ergo, nobody really knows who coined the phrase, and it becomes something similar in nature to statistics about gun ownership, concealed carry and violent crime. Nobody can be certain.

Critics of such research will point to what another researcher, David Hemenway, director of the Harvard Injury Control Research Center and a professor at the Harvard School of Public Health acknowledged in an Op-Ed piece that appeared in the Los Angeles Times: "Of course it's possible to find researchers who side with the NRA in believing that guns make our society safer, rather than more dangerous. As I've shown, however, they're in the minority.

"Scientific consensus isn't always right," Hemenway added, "but it's our best guide to understanding the world. Can reporters please stop pretending that scientists, like politicians, are evenly divided on guns? We're not."

But all of this statistical discussion aside, the public is still arming up, and increasing numbers of people are carrying firearms outside of the home for personal protection, especially in the aftermath of San Bernardino.

Note what Judge Richard Posner of the Seventh Circuit Court of Appeals said when he wrote the decision overturning the Illinois ban on carry in *Moore v. Madigan*: "Twenty-first century Illinois has no hostile Indians. But a Chicagoan is a good deal more likely to be attacked on a sidewalk in a rough neighborhood than in his apartment on the 35th floor of the Park Tower. A woman who is being stalked or has obtained a protective order against a violent ex-husband is more vulnerable to being attacked while walking to or from her home than when inside. She has a stronger self-defense claim to be allowed to carry a gun in public than the resident of a fancy apartment building (complete with doorman) has a claim to sleep with a loaded gun under her mattress."

Like the woman in Judge Posner's opinion, it is the concern for what might happen out on the street more than what might occur inside the home that convinces people to take responsibility for their own safety and self-preservation.

One vivid example of this need to defend one's self outside the home was a highly-publicized unprovoked attack on a visibly-armed private citizen in the east-central Washington community of Yakima, to be discussed in greater detail in Chapter Four. This man was shopping in a Wal-Mart with his son for some baseball equipment and he was legally carrying a pistol in full view.

Quite suddenly, he was attacked by another man who grabbed a metal baseball bat and swung it at his head, but hit him instead on the shoulder.

This sort of news report is not uncommon, with what appears to be an increasing number of homeless and often mentally disturbed people living untreated or with little treatment in American communities, large and small. This sort of story can also be linked to a rise in gang activity and associated "initiations" that may include playing the notorious "Knock Out Game" of randomly approaching strangers from the rear and punching them into unconsciousness with a blow to the head.

It is more than that, as noted earlier. People concerned about legislative attempts to erode their gun rights will not meekly surrender to the desires of gun prohibitionists. They will do quite the opposite.

An editorial in the Tyler, Texas *Morning Telegraph* during the debate on whether the open carry of sidearms should be legalized in the Lone Star State perhaps put the most clarity to the controversy by noting, "When it comes to rights, polls don't matter. Rights are rights, whether popular or unpopular. They're derived from our Creator, not from popular consent."

This was in reaction to a poll conducted by the University of Texas and Texas Tribune that found "Most Texas voters support the right to carry guns in public, but a large majority would not allow open carry of those weapons with or without licenses."

The Tyler newspaper editorial slammed down pretty hard by concluding, "It doesn't matter what the majority thinks, the Second Amendment enumerates a basic right — the right to defense of self and property. That right was most recently reiterated in the U.S. Supreme Court's 2008 Heller decision…What the Texas Legislature is debating now isn't whether we have such a right, but how Texans should be able to express that right. It's not about popular opinions."

Millions and counting

Swimming against the tide, as it were – at least the prevailing scientific tide described by Hemenway and his contemporaries – is Dr. John Lott, president of the Crime Prevention Research Center and the author of several books related to guns and crime, including the well-received (in firearms circles, anyway) *More Guns = Less Crime*. Lott is an economist and he is very good with numbers and statistics.

His latest estimate on the number of American citizens licensed to carry across the 50 states is above 12 million. His research is in sharp contrast, if not contradiction, to the findings of Donohue, Hemenway and others. In an interview with Fox News, Lott asserted, "When you allow people to carry concealed handguns, you see changes in the behavior of criminals."

Before anyone dismisses that as poppycock, there is considerable anecdotal evidence that suggests Lott is onto something. According to Lott and the Fox report, "The real measure of the deterrent effect of concealed carry permits is not laws on the books but the percentage of a given state's population that holds the permits."

"In 10 states," Fox reported, "more than 8 percent of adults hold concealed carry permits, and all are among the states with the lowest crime rates. Lott claims his group's analysis shows that each one percentage point increase in the adult population holding permits brings a 1.4 percent drop in the murder rate.

"We found that the size of the drop (in crime) is directly related to the percentage of the population with permits," Lott said, according to the Fox News report.

Lott is a Fox News contributor, and he further asserted that some criminals simply stop committing crimes, or they move to other areas where they might be less likely to be shot by an intended victim, something nationally-recognized firearms and self-defense expert Massad Ayoob has called "A fatal error in the victim-selection process." No criminal intent on becoming a recidivist is going to risk getting shot if he knows an intended victim is armed and capable of using a firearm in self-defense.

What is significant about Lott's estimate on the number of concealed carry permit/license holders is that back in 2011, the U.S. Government Accountability office "found that 8 million Americans held them," Fox reported. That's quite a spike over the course of four years, but it might be easily illustrated by what happened in a single state, Washington, which is often considered a "Blue" state because of the way its national election results have trended.

At the end of 2012, the Washington Department of Licensing told the authors that there were 392,784 active concealed pistol licenses. Two years later, on the last day of 2014, the DOL reported 478,460 active CPLs. That's an increase of 85,676 carry licenses, an average of more than 42,000 new licenses per year, and the trend has been continuing upwards.

Apply this phenomenon to all the other states with "shall-issue" laws, meaning that anyone who passes a background check can obtain a carry license, and it is without question that more people are going armed, or at least going through the process to be legally armed.

Florida has the most concealed carry licenses, and Texas comes in at Number 2. When Fox news checked, the combined total of licensed citizens in just those two states was approximately two million.

According to the NSSF, a growing segment of the armed populace are female. That organization's research indicates that 26 percent of women purchasing firearms are doing so for self-defense, followed closely by those buying guns for home defense. It would hardly be a stretch of the imagination to suggest that eventually, many of the women buying guns for home defense will ultimately obtain a license to carry.

Fully one-third of respondents to a survey conducted for NSSF by the Chicago-based InfoManiacs were first-time gun owners, a statistic that might cause some consternation to the anti-gun lobby, which has argued unconvincingly that fewer people are buying guns. Another thing the NSSF survey revealed, as reported by the *Houston Chronicle*, was that these women were pretty seriously invested. They spent an average of $870 on firearms, and these are not "impulse" purchases. The survey found that 67 percent of the respondents had spent a few months considering their purchase and 65 percent had talked about it with a family member.

Thirty-two percent of those women said they go target shooting at least once a month, and some 3.3 million women go hunting, the newspaper reported, quoting a 2013 statistic from the National Sporting Goods Association.

Another anecdotal report in the *Detroit Free Press* noted that the number of women obtaining carry licenses in Michigan had more than doubled over a four-year period dating backwards from 2014. That newspaper said several gun shops and ranges offer women-only courses and that they are "often full."

The *Free Press* quoted one woman who had a gun because she works at night and "doesn't feel safe walking to her car." That is a concern shared by a lot of people who work odd hours, and not necessarily all of them are female.

Likewise, the *Minneapolis Star Tribune* reported a record number of Minnesotans who are legally armed, using data for 2014 – the most recent information available at this writing – to note an increase of more than 14 percent in the number of carry permits over the previous year.

The newspaper quoted the Crime Prevention Research Center's estimate that about 3.95 percent of adults in the state were licensed to carry. The Center, according to the story, had determined that "states with a high percentage of gun ownership often had low violent-crime rates. Murder rates dropped 22 percent nationally from 2007 to 2013, while the adult population with weapons permits jumped 130 percent over the same period."

Whether it is the publicized surge in concealed carry, or a combination of factors as suggested by Tod Burke, whom Fox News identified as a criminal justice professor at Radford University in Virginia, and a former police officer, it makes the armed citizen feel safer, and can enable such citizens to defend themselves against violent crime. A few highly-publicized self-defense shootings can have a causal effect on the decline in willingness of street thugs to attack people.

Why gun control proponents stubbornly refuse to acknowledge this is perhaps one reason why the gun control movement has been losing traction over the years, even with events such as the Sandy Hook tragedy. The concept of gun control may be more amenable following attacks like the one in Newtown, but it has not been a lasting idea with any staying power among the American people.

In early 2015, Pew Research released a startling report that there had been something of a sea change in the attitudes of Americans about firearms. Based on a survey in December 2014, Pew revealed that, for the first time, "more Americans say that protecting gun rights is more important than controlling gun ownership" by a margin of 52 percent to 46 percent. In some elections, that would be considered a landslide disparity.

Even more significant was the overwhelming shift in the public attitude about having guns in the home. Pew, alluding to a Gallup poll in October 2014, noted that 63 percent of Americans believe having a gun in the home makes them safer, while 30 percent think homes with guns are more dangerous. This was an eyebrow-raising reversal of a similar survey 15 years prior, that found 51 percent of Americans questioned believed that guns in the home made them less safe, while only 35 percent thought guns made a home safer.

Perhaps not so surprising was something else the Gallup survey revealed. Republicans (81%) are nearly twice as likely to believe guns in the home make it safer than Democrats (41%), according to Gallup. This tends to amplify the earlier suggestion that Democrats are more supportive of gun control.

Quoting Gallup, there was one other finding worthy of note: "Although there is a gender gap in the results for this question, majorities of both men (67%) and women (58%) believe having a gun improves home safety. While one in three women say it makes for a more dangerous place to be, only one in four men say the same about guns in the home."

The *Washington Examiner* covered this story, noting that the shift came almost exactly two years after President Obama had pushed for gun control measures following the Sandy Hook tragedy. Perhaps the Pew report explained how all of this had happened.

"We are at a moment when most Americans believe crime rates are rising and when most believe gun ownership – not gun control – makes people safer," Pew said. "In the 1990s, the rate of violent crimes plummeted by more than half nationwide. Public perceptions tracked right along, with the share saying there was more crime in the U.S. over the past year falling from 87 percent in 1993 to just 41 percent by 2001. In the new century, however, there's been a disconnect. A majority of Americans (63%) said in a Gallup survey last year that crime was on the rise, despite crime statistics holding near 20-year lows."

Even Pew could not explain what the *Washington Examiner* called "this disconnect." It could be the fault of news coverage ("If it bleeds, it leads") or a combination of sensationalized bad news, reality television and political rhetoric, Pew suggested.

Why are people carrying?

More light might be shed on why increasing numbers of Americans are getting carry permits by looking at an interesting website Concealedguns.procon.org. This site presented pros and cons of concealed carry from the perspectives of those supporting and opposing the carry of firearms by private citizens.

Arguments on both sides are fairly typical, and in some cases, amount to "boilerplate" with little more than opinion based on emotion to back them up. On the "pro" side of the equation, people argue that concealed handguns deter crime and that "responsible citizens should have the right to arm themselves against criminals with guns. They cited an analysis by the aforementioned John Lott that suggested states with "shall-issue" concealed carry laws had seen a decline in murders of 8.5 percent, aggravated assaults by seven percent and rapes by five percent.

On the "con" side, the arguments were similarly couched. Allowing concealed handguns increases crime, they contend, along with the chance that simple arguments could escalate into something deadly. That side contended that states with "shall issue" laws saw an increase in the murder rate of two percent or more, and a nine percent increase of rape and aggravated assault.

And here we have an example of what Prof. Donohue explained. Different statistical models can produce different results.

Which side is right? That appears to depend upon one's personal perspective about armed self-defense and the Second Amendment. Those who believe in exercising their right to keep and bear arms – as more people appear to be doing – will subscribe to the "pro" position and those who advocate for stricter gun controls, or gun bans altogether, will gravitate toward the "con" arguments as though they were gospel.

One of the "con" arguments listed on the Concealedguns.procon.org website was this: "Public safety should be left to professionally qualified police officers, not private citizens with little or no expert training." As concealed and open carry advocates will observe, that philosophy is just swell, provided there is a police officer at the scene of a crime as it unfolds, but how often does that really happen? It is a very rare crime that occurs when a cop is close enough to intervene and stop it. When an armed citizen is able to act, as has happened at a few mass shooting incidents, that person is the "first responder," not the police or sheriff's deputy who responds to the call.

The one "con" argument that is most likely to leave Second Amendment activists shaking their heads and rolling their eyes is this: "Concealed weapons laws make the non-carrying public feel less safe."

This has to rank among the stupidest arguments; one suggestive that anti-gunners are simply paranoid about the desire of their fellow citizens to defend themselves against violent crime by fighting back. It may also reflect what the late Col. Jeff Cooper, deemed by many to be the "father of modern pistolcraft," called "hoplophobia."

Cooper explained this term, which he invented, in one of his commentaries: "I coined the term...in 1962 in response to a perceived need for a word to describe a mental aberration consisting of an unreasoning terror of gadgetry, specifically, weapons. The most common manifestation of hoplophobia is the idea that instruments possess a will of their own, apart from that of their user. This is not a reasoned position, but when you point this out to a hoplophobe he is not impressed because his is an unreasonable position. To convince a man that he is not making sense is not to change his viewpoint but rather to make an enemy. Thus hoplophobia is a useful word, but as with all words, it should be used correctly."

In short, the term, while not alluding to a genuinely recognized phobia, applies to those with an unnatural fear of firearms.

Over the years as the gun control debate has unfolded, it has become something of an expectation to see members of the clergy weigh in on the side of the anti-gun crowd. Church groups were heavily involved in a Washington State initiative campaign to pass a so-called "universal background check" law that was actually a rather poorly disguised handgun registration scheme.

But one Catholic priest in Ann Arbor, Michigan made headlines when he encouraged his parishioners to arm up. He went a step farther by holding concealed pistol license classes at his church, according to a story publicized online by the *Daily Caller* and reported by the *Detroit Free Press*.

The Rev. Edward Fride even took some criticism from the Bishop of Lansing, Earl Boyea, according to one report, and some parishioners who didn't care for his pro-gun stance. The Bishop called the classes "inappropriate activities" for Church property, and in a statement from the Diocese of Lansing to the Detroit newspaper, he said he had never granted permission to anyone to carry a concealed handgun in a Diocese church or school.

To justify his position, Rev. Fride noted that Detroit Police Chief James Craig had recently suggested that citizens in his city arm themselves against crime.

Well, when police and a priest say it's okay, it must be okay, right?

It should be noted for the record that Fride had to back away from his proposal, but not before the idea had at least gotten a lot of people talking about firearms and self-defense.

Be careful where you carry

Perhaps the biggest problem to emerge from the concealed carry surge is the inexplicable stupidity of a relative handful of people who try to carry guns where they should not, and even more egregiously walk through an airport terminal security checkpoint with a gun in their carry-on bag. The "I forgot it was there" argument gets rather stale after all of the years these checkpoints have been in operation. After all, people are supposed to examine their carry-ons before going to the airport, aren't they? People approaching a scanner ought to know better, shouldn't they?

Fortunately, the overwhelming majority of people who travel with firearms do it responsibly and by the rules. Thanks to an increasing number of states with reciprocity agreements that recognize the concealed carry licenses and permits of other states, the major airlines are well aware that people are taking firearms along on trips to friendly environs. That does not include New York, New Jersey, Hawaii and a few other states that do not recognize out-of-state carry permits. New York and New Jersey are infamous for arresting travelers with guns in their luggage when they declare them at the ticket/check-in counter, as required.

Armed citizens who travel should always check the local laws in the area to which they are headed, so they do not run afoul of a statute or regulation that is unlike what one lives with at home.

There are a couple of very good resources at hand. The website Handgunlaw.us is regularly updated with information on local laws and concealed carry reciprocity. There is also an annual publication called the *Traveler's Guide*, a magazine-sized book with one-page briefs on the laws of all the 50 states.

In general, there are some places where concealed carry is not allowed in any state, and these are pretty easy to remember. They include federal government facilities such as federal office buildings and courthouses, military posts and bases. This includes post offices and U.S. Forest Service ranger stations.

It is legal to carry in national parks and on federal lands controlled by the Bureau of Land Management, and in national forests, *all subject to state laws.*

Depending upon the state, one may or may not carry in state government facilities including state legislative office buildings and the state capitol, and courthouses. Hospitals, whether public or private, are also high on the list of places where firearms are typically not allowed.

Public school campuses and colleges and universities in most states also prohibit firearms, although this could be slowly changing.

A particular state's law may also preclude someone from having a firearm in a restaurant where alcohol is served, while others allow people to carry, so long as they don't consume alcoholic beverages.

And there are provisions in many states that allow private businesses to prohibit firearms on their premises. Some gun control groups have pressured such businesses to bar firearms. In Seattle several years ago, then-Mayor Mike McGinn, an anti-gun member of Michael Bloomberg's Mayors Against Illegal Guns, initiated an election year program with a local gun control group that encouraged restaurants and other establishments to declare their premises "gun-free" zones. The prohibition had no force of law, but in that state, if an armed citizen is asked to leave and they don't, they can then be arrested for criminal trespass.

It is incumbent upon the individual citizen to do a bit of research before making a foolish mistake that could cost someone his/her carry permit or license, and even result in a criminal conviction.

On the plus side, the more people decide to arm themselves and apply for a carry license or permit, the more they are researching this subject. The Internet has been something of a boon for this endeavor, because in the midst of all the nutty things one finds in cyberspace, there is also a wealth of good, reliable information.

Some of these resources are put together by extremely dedicated people who do not taint their information with a personal political bias. Their matter-of-fact approach is educational and they provide information that quite possibly would not otherwise be available.

Yet, it is the occasional person with either a memory lapse or who is careless that gets the occasional headline about trying to carry a gun through a security checkpoint at an airport. Education prevents or cures most of these cases, which at times have involved some rather prominent people including politicians and professional athletes.

Armed citizens matter

With all of these millions of armed citizens in our midst, one might expect there to be daily news reports of some person stopping a horrible crime. That's how gun control proponents couch the conversation, as if to suggest armed self-defense never happens, or occurs so rarely as to be irrelevant, thus not providing justification for carrying a gun.

In fact, there are frequent reports of legally-armed citizens stopping crimes either by fighting back against a direct attack or by intervention in a crime committed against someone else. Such reports have been the basis for one of the most popular features on the KeepandBearArms.com website appropriately dubbed "Operation Self-Defense."

The argument that legally-armed citizens are not involved in that many defensive incidents is demonstrably false.

Rather than devote an entire chapter to anecdotes involving armed citizens, it is important that such cases be considered not as the way things ought to be, but a direct result of things as the way they are. These otherwise ordinary individuals were prepared when they suddenly found themselves in extraordinary situations.

Anti-self-defense advocates have lately taken to narrowing down their argument, intimating that no armed citizen has ever stopped a mass shooting. Again, that is not the case and only cursory research would confirm as much.

One such incident unfolded in a hospital near Philadelphia, Pa., in July 2014. Dr. Lee Silverman is lucky to have had a defensive sidearm in his office at Mercy Fitzgerald Hospital in the community of Yeadon. Yes, it is a "gun-free zone," but that did not stop the would-be mass shooter who came into the facility and opened fire. Killed almost outright was caseworker Theresa Hunt, who – according to an account in the *Christian Science Monitor* – had brought the gunman to the hospital for treatment.

Dr. Silverman was grazed on the head by a bullet, but that didn't stop him from shooting the attacker several times, seriously wounding the man, who was taken into custody and later charged.

Various published reports say Silverman's colleagues were surprised he was armed. That's really the way it is supposed to be. As many a concealed carry instructor has advised, nobody in your presence should know you are carrying a gun. Discretion leads to nasty surprises for would-be killers and other criminals.

Yeadon Police Chief Donald Molineux was quoted by various media observing, "If he (Silverman) wasn't armed ... this guy could have went out in the hallway and just walked down the offices until he ran out of ammunition."

People who carry always or frequently insist they are not eager to use a firearm in self-defense, but they are even less obliging to the idea of being a victim. They have decided to fight back, even if it means – as may have been the case with Dr. Silverman – doing so in defiance of 'no-gun" policies that always seem to disarm law-abiding citizens, but never the people intent on killing them.

By no small coincidence, another shooting in Philadelphia in March 2015 underscored the necessity of being armed at the right time. A man identified as Warren Edwards became embroiled in some sort of altercation with the operator of a barber shop in West Philadelphia. At the time, there were several people in the shop, including children.

A report carried by the *Daily Caller* said Edwards drew a gun after a barber told him to "chill out," and started shooting. At that moment, a customer who had just walked into the shop drew his own licensed firearm and shot Edwards in the chest, felling him and stopping what police later suggested could have been carnage.

A police spokesman, Capt. Frank Llewellyn, told reporters that the legally-armed citizen "responded and I guess he saved a lot of people in there."

The man reportedly ran from the shop but later showed up at a police precinct to surrender.

And then there was the case of Everardo Custodio, the 22-year-old who opened fire on a group of Chicagoans at Logan Square, only to discover that an Uber driver parked there had his own, legally-carried handgun, with which he shot Custodio several times. The gunman was taken to a local hospital and treated for wounds to the leg and lower back, according to the *Chicago Tribune*.

This was an interesting case for the Second Amendment Foundation, because it was their federal lawsuit, and the similar legal action by the National Rifle Association mentioned at the beginning of this chapter, that had forced Illinois lawmakers about 20 months earlier to adopt a concealed carry law. Illinois was the last state in the country, stubbornly holding out to the bitter end, to allow legal concealed carry.

The Uber driver was licensed and legally armed. The gun he used was one of a generation of defensive handguns chambered for both the .45 Colt cartridge and the .410 shotgun shell. Such revolvers are made by Smith & Wesson and Taurus, for just such self-defense and defense-of-others situations.

By some estimates, armed citizens defend themselves with firearms – usually without a shot being fired – as many as 2.5 million times a year, but even if the number is far less than that, the principle of the gun ban zealots applies: "If it saves *just one* life, it's worth it."

Pare down that estimate to only those who defend themselves away from home or business; that is, with a legally-carried firearm, and one still has an impressive number of incidents in which the presence of a gun made the difference.

The public has recognized that law enforcement is stretched thin, and sometimes to the limit. People want to be safe, and that goes beyond just feeling safe, they want to assure their safety with the tools that give them a fighting chance against criminal attack.

They are exercising their constitutionally-affirmed civil right to *bear* arms by legally carrying defensive sidearms. There is no indication that this trend will slow down anytime soon. Anyone attempting to curtail this right does so at his or her own political peril.

Wildlife benefits

One thing rarely touched on in the battle to protect Second Amendment rights is the financial benefit derived from gun ownership. This plays particularly well in the public forum, as there is no way that the gun prohibition lobby can financially match what gun owners, whether they are hunters, target ore recreational shooters, or individuals interested in personal protection have contributed to wildlife management, thanks to a sportsman-supported measure called the Pittman-Robertson Federal Aid to Wildlife Restoration program, created in the 1930s.

For some 80 years, the Pittman-Robertson special federal excise tax on firearms and ammunition, and archery equipment, has resulted in billions of dollars in revenue that supports both federal and state wildlife programs. That money is managed as a dedicated fund by the U.S. Fish & Wildlife Service, and a large part of it is annually apportioned to state fish and wildlife agencies for use in wildlife management.

For example, the most recent data available at this writing showed that for Fiscal Year 2015, Pittman-Robertson provided $808,492,189 that was divided among the states. For example, Pennsylvania, a state rich in the hunting and gun-owning tradition, received more than $29 million, Michigan was allocated more than $26.5 million, Wisconsin got more than $24.8 million and Montana received more than $21.5 million.

These apportionments not only help pay the freight for wildlife management – both game and non-game species – but also support hunter education programs, the source of much firearms safety education for many adults and youth, and in some cases range development. Some state hunter education programs rely heavily on these funds to operate, so when gun prohibitionists complain about the money spent on guns and ammunition, such arguments can be answered with hard facts about what those sales support.

More than $8.4 *billion* has been distributed to the states since 1939. Thanks to state matching funds, these added revenues have been used to purchase wildlife habitat that is open to all the public, not just hunters and shooters. They have helped wildlife restoration programs that returned elk, wild turkey and other populations to regions where they may have once thrived, but had long ago vanished.

A lot of people who own firearms and have never even considered hunting contribute to this fund. There have been some recent years when the fund has skyrocketed, largely because of gun control efforts and pronouncements that sent people scurrying to gun shops and sporting goods stores to buy whatever it was they thought might be restricted or banned. It was no joke when gun owners and even some industry insiders observed that Presidents Bill Clinton and Barack Obama have been "the best gun salesmen in history."

By threatening to curtail gun ownership, extremists in the gun control movement can be called out for the harm their agenda would do to wildlife, from songbirds to grizzly bears.

2: LEGISLATING ON A CIVIL RIGHT

"Like most rights, the right secured by the Second Amendment is not unlimited." – Supreme Court Justice Antonin Scalia, *District of Columbia v. Dick Anthony Heller,* June 2008

Writing for the U.S. Supreme Court majority in the landmark 2008 decision in *District of Columbia v. Dick Anthony Heller,* the late Associate Justice Antonin Scalia made it clear – contrary to what people on both sides of the Second Amendment argument believe at the extremes that the right to keep and bear arms is either, a) absolute, or b) a collective right of the states to form militias – that the amendment affirms and protects an individual civil right, but that this right is not without limits.

Just as nobody can claim First Amendment protection for slander, libel or yelling "Fire!" in a crowded theater (unless, of course, there actually is a fire), the right to keep and bear arms, as Scalia explained, referring to Blackstone and subsequent discussions and court rulings, "was not a right to keep and carry any weapon whatsoever in any manner whatsoever and for whatever purpose."

The right to bear arms does not protect boorish or intimidating behavior, nor does it protect the promiscuous use of firearms in such a manner that the public safety is endangered. You are not allowed to discharge firearms in the air, in a public park at midnight on New Year's Eve or the Fourth of July, for example. You may not intimidate people with a firearm, nor engage in other careless behavior that results in injury or death and claim some uninfringeable right to keep and bear arms under the Second Amendment as a defense, or an excuse. We will discuss this at length in a later chapter.

Further, Justice Scalia observed, "Although we do not undertake an exhaustive historical analysis...of the full scope of the Second Amendment, nothing in our opinion should be taken to cast doubt on longstanding prohibitions on the possession of firearms by felons and the mentally ill, or laws forbidding the carrying of firearms in sensitive places such as schools and government buildings, or laws imposing conditions and qualifications on the commercial sale of arms..."

On the other hand, writing a few pages later in his majority opinion, Scalia also made it abundantly clear that such regulation cannot be so restrictive in its nature as to essentially prohibit the exercise of Second Amendment rights, especially if it involves what amounts to a ban on an entire class of firearms, in this case, handguns.

"It is no answer to say," Justice Scalia explained, "that it is permissible to ban the possession of handguns so long as the possession of other firearms (*i.e.,* long guns) is allowed. It is enough to note, as we have observed, that the American people have considered the handgun to be the quintessential self-defense weapon. There are many reasons that a citizen may prefer a handgun for home defense: It is easier to store in a location that is readily accessible in an emergency; it cannot easily be redirected or wrestled away by an attacker; it is easier to use for those without the upper-body strength to lift and aim a long gun; it can be pointed at a burglar with one hand while the other hand dials the police. Whatever the reason, handguns are the most popular weapon chosen by Americans for self-defense in the home, and a complete prohibition of their use is invalid."

State legislatures have long been considered as having the authority to regulate the carry and use of firearms within their state borders. In many states over the past 25 years, so-called "state preemption" statutes have been adopted for the purpose of statewide gun law uniformity. That is, what is legal in one part of a state is legal in another part, and no local jurisdiction may adopt ordinances or regulations that exceed state law.

With the June 2010 Supreme Court ruling in *Mc-Donald v. City of Chicago*, authored by Associate Justice Samuel Alito, the Second Amendment was incorporated to the states via the Fourteenth Amendment. It has opened the door for such organizations as the Second Amendment Foundation (SAF), which brought the *McDonald* case to the high court, and National Rifle Association (NRA) to begin a series of legal challenges to certain offensive state and local laws and regulations that violate the Second Amendment.

Legislatures, while they pay attention to court rulings, occasionally try to "push the envelope" as it were, adopting statutes that essentially probe the edges of court dictum, perhaps to see what they can get away with. This is particularly true with the right to keep and bear arms, and such legislative activism pre-dates both *Heller* and *McDonald* by many years.

As celebrated author Samuel Langhorne Clemens – a.k.a. Mark Twain – once observed, "No man's life, liberty, or property are safe while the legislature is in session." The quote is also attributed to 19th Century attorney and newspaper editor Gideon John Tucker. Conservatives and Second Amendment advocates will insist both were correct.

It is not so common today as it may have been two decades ago to find the activism all going in one direction, that is, to ratchet down on the right to keep and bear arms. In recent years, legislatures have actually adopted new laws or reformed existing statutes that are friendlier to the Second Amendment. But this is not universal, and even when lawmakers adopt favorable statutes, a governor can veto the measures.

One example was the veto by West Virginia Gov. Earl Ray Tomblin in early 2015 of a controversial measure to eliminate the requirement for a citizen to obtain a state concealed carry permit. This would have led to what activists in the Second Amendment community call "constitutional carry," and it will be discussed in greater detail in Chapter Five.

Tomblin's veto created something of a shockwave in West Virginia. The Mountain State is considered to be "gun country," and the governor has enjoyed high ratings from the NRA. This time around, however, he nixed the measure, and gave this statement to the *Charleston Daily Mail:* "Throughout my career, I have strongly supported the Second Amendment, as demonstrated by my repeated endorsements and high grades from the National Rifle Association. However, I must also be responsive to the apprehension of law enforcement officers from across the state, who have concerns about the bill as it relates to the safety of their fellow officers. It also would eliminate the required gun safety training courses for those applying for a concealed carry permit. In light of these concerns and in the interest of public safety for all West Virginians, I have vetoed Senate Bill 347."

At times like this, many gun rights activists argue that law enforcement should not have what they say appears to be veto authority over legislation that expands their right to bear arms.

Indeed, the use of law enforcement support or opposition to legislative proposals from the White House on down has become something of political theater in most cases. This has been particularly so when the president or a governor has appeared before a group of peace officers promoting some effort, as if to create the impression that the measure had law enforcement support.

Gun control proponents *love* to have cops standing in the background when they make some announcement. The individual officers don't necessarily enjoy it, and there have been alleged instances when pro-gun police complained about having to be essentially a political prop for a photo-op.

There are also instances where rank-and-file officers or sheriff's deputies have been at odds with their bosses on gun-related issues, though it is less common where county sheriffs are concerned because they are elected, while police chiefs are appointed by mayors who are often anti-gun liberals.

On the other hand, Kansas Gov. Sam Brownback did sign such legislation about the same time, making the Sunflower State the sixth state to allow carry without a permit, as noted by the *Kansas City Star*. Under this new law, permits will still be issued for those who wish to exercise their rights under reciprocity agreements with many other states that recognize non-resident licenses and permits.

Unlike his West Virginia colleague, Brownback noted in a statement, "We're saying that if you want to do that in this state, then you don't have to get the permission slip from the government. It is a constitutional right, and we're removing a barrier to that right."

And, like it or not, opponents of the measure had their say in print, and it was predictable "blood-in-the-streets" rhetoric. Senator Oletha Faust-Goudeau (D-Wichita) perhaps revealed too much about her personal feeling toward legally-armed citizens when she told the newspaper, "That's a major responsibility to carry a gun, whether it's concealed or not. And it's scary…I predict from the legislation that — and it's going to go quick, it's going to be July 1 — we're going to see some accidents, possibly deaths."

This is why nothing is a "slam-dunk" in any state legislature when it comes to firearms, even in gun-friendly states.

The D.C. dilemma

In early spring 2015 in the days leading up to his announced bid for the Republican nomination for president in 2016, Florida Sen. Marco Rubio and Republican Ohio Congressman Jim Jordan announced legislation aimed at easing the gun control laws in the District of Columbia. Some people, including vehemently anti-gun and ultra-liberal D.C. Delegate Eleanor Holmes Norton, saw this as simply a political ploy designed to strengthen Rubio's conservative credentials for the presidential campaign.

However, others in the gun rights movement saw Rubio's Second Amendment Enforcement Act of 2015 as a legitimate reaction to the onerous gun control laws adopted by the District in the wake of the 2008 *Heller* ruling. A bureau chief for the *Tampa Bay Times* suggested at the time that the legislation "has little chance of becoming reality."

According to the newspaper's account, Rubio's measure would essentially prevent the D.C. city council from enacting "restrictive gun control measures." In addition, it would repeal the city's registration system, allow District residents to purchase firearms from licensed dealers in both Virginia and Maryland, and mandate that the city's permits would become "shall issue" documents for anyone legally able to own and carry a firearm, taking away the discretionary authority of the government to deny a permit based on little more than a whim.

True as that may be, introducing the measure did bring a little temporary attention to the situation in the nation's capital. While the city had been compelled by the courts, thanks to a SAF lawsuit, to create some form of concealed carry ordinance, they crafted it to be as restrictive and bureaucratic as possible, so as to discourage citizens from applying.

This is often what legislation at the state level is designed to accomplish. For the anti-self-defense crowd, any provision that keeps people from exercising their rights is a good thing, the Constitution be damned. Whether it is the imposition of so-called "universal background checks" to a licensing program that requires a lengthy application process and some proof of "need" as determined by a police chief or some other official, discouraging people from carrying firearms in public for their personal safety is paramount to many in the gun prohibition lobby.

Illinois lawmakers were nearly as bad in putting together that state's concealed carry statute, complete with a training requirement. It's not necessarily the same thing as a "literacy test" that might have been used to discourage southern blacks from voting, but it follows the same principle. The more offensive bureaucratic hoop is the discretionary issue provision in the District.

One legislative truth that many in the gun rights movement do not seem to grasp is that it is never an easy proposition to push through a pro- or anti-gun law, and one cannot simply declare that a particular proposal should become law just by saying so. Not every lawmaker is a friend to the Second Amendment, and they seem to demonstrate that with every new legislative session by blocking this or that bill. Nothing is guaranteed from any legislative body.

For example, Wyoming lawmakers rejected a concealed carry expansion measure in 2015 that would have allowed citizens with a concealed weapons permit to carry defensive firearms on school campuses, sporting events and even into the legislature. When the brother of Wyoming Gov. Matt Mead came out against the measure, his opposition was detailed in a guest opinion column that appeared in the *Jackson Hole News and Guide*. And he couched his opposition with this:

> "The law enforcement community around the state isn't unanimous in its view of House Bill 114, but I've spoken with Sheriff Jim Whalen, who is a supporter of the Second Amendment but is against this bill. He's worried about the difficulty of-

ficers arriving at a shooting will have telling John Wayne(s) from the bad guy. And, I suspect, he has to worry a bit about the ability of non-law-enforcement folks knowing when lethal force is appropriate.

"I agree with Patricia Nichols, the Teton County School Board chairwoman. If school safety is truly the goal, the Legislature can do far better by funding school safety officers. But this bill isn't about safety. And it's not about the constitution. It's grounded in a vague philosophical hysteria that limiting firearms at college football games somehow undermines the republic.

"I hunt. I've had to shoot dogs that bit, horses caught in wire and cows with broken legs. I'll compare my arsenal to anyone's, but I don't need to carry it with me to the school play."

When gun owners are divided on a measure, its chances of survival even in a pro-gun legislature are reduced, so when bad laws are proposed that get support from some gun owners, or when good laws are opposed by some gun owners, division often results in doom. And gun activists have been seemingly unable to grasp the simple truth that urban populations – even in western states – are inclined to vote liberal/Democrat and send anti-gunners to the state capitol, while voters in rural areas tend to send pro-gun conservative Republicans, but they are sometimes outnumbered.

Nowhere has this been more visible in recent memory than in Colorado, Washington and Oregon. Those three states have elected anti-gun majorities to state legislatures, sometimes by narrow margins of course, but when anti-gunners control the legislative agenda and committee assignments and chairs, it's easy to see who loses.

Far too many gun votes are along party lines. Colorado and Oregon have proven that, as have legislatures in several other states.

Washington was a slightly different situation with its Initiative 594 campaign in 2014. The measure passed for several reasons, not the least of which was the heavy spending by the gun prohibition lobby. To pass the so-called "universal background check" measure, anti-gunners spent $10.2 million against barely one-fifth that amount spent by the firearms community.

Worse still, some gun owners actually voted for the measure (many later regretting it, but stubbornly refusing to acknowledge the mistake they had made), and far too many other gun owners didn't bother to vote. Apathy is as responsible for the erosion of Second Amendment rights as outright attacks by the gun control lobby.

Offering up the excuse that "my vote doesn't matter" or "it's all rigged anyway" amounts to automatic failure. Someone else does your voting for you, and it's typically against your interests.

Making good law

There are times when legislatures can accomplish something positive. In Ohio, for example, lawmakers improved state law in 2015 to allow hunters to use suppressors, while allowing Buckeye firearms owners the opportunity to buy rifles and shotguns from any state, as detailed by the *Columbus Dispatch*. This same legislation contained another benefit to gun owners. Training requirements were reduced in order to qualify for a concealed carry permit.

Another tenet to the new law is recognition of non-resident concealed carry permits and licenses, the newspaper reported.

As Jim Irvine, chairman of the Buckeye Firearms Association, put it, "Over time, people will look back and see this as a watershed law that fixed a lot of little things."

Think about that for a minute. No bill is ever going to provide the be-all, end-all on gun rights. Those who insist on "all or nothing" from a piece of legislation are invariably going to wind up with nothing. While "nothing" may be advertised as some kind of victory, it is often quite the opposite. Nothing was really lost in Ohio, and there were some small gains.

That much was immediately obvious by the reaction from the leader of an Ohio gun control group, who was quoted by the newspaper arguing, "There are a number of troubling provisions in the bill. There's nothing for us to celebrate in this bill." When an anti-gunner says that, it's time to throw a party.

Revisions to the Ohio law are good for every legally-armed citizen who may travel to that state and desire to carry for personal protection. One's right of self-defense does not end at a state border, and laws that recognize out-of-state licenses and permits – so long as the armed citizen operates under the laws of Ohio while in the state – can only help in the long run.

Even in New York, a state considered by many to be overly restrictive where guns are concerned, some good things can happen legislatively. An effort to ban .50-caliber rifles was killed in a state Senate committee, with predictable reactions from gun control proponents.

In reporting the story, the *Albany Times Union* noted that it was a Republican-controlled Senate Codes Committee that killed the legislation on a 9-7 vote. Recall what we said earlier about legislative control making the difference on what legislation passes and what does not.

Like Ohio and several other states, Washington lawmakers changed state law a few years ago to allow the possession and use of silencers. Prior to that, people could actually own the sound suppression devices and even mount them on firearms, but could not shoot the guns on which they were installed. How senseless is that?

Changing the law to allow use of suppressors was supported by law enforcement, and signed into law by former Gov. Christine Gregoire, a Democrat.

Another Second Amendment-friendly state is Mississippi. Gov. Phil Bryant had promised to sign legislation that lowered the cost of a carry permit, and protected controversial "green tip" ammunition that had been targeted by the Obama administration because it was suddenly deemed to be "armor piercing" – in contradiction to long-standing policy and statutory exemption – by the Bureau of Alcohol, Tobacco, Firearms and Explosives.

Long story short here is that firearms are subject to some regulation, regardless what anyone may wish or honestly believe. There are ample court precedents affirming the authority of state and even local governments to impose some rules, not necessarily on firearms as instruments, but on the behavior of people who own and use them.

It is possible to narrowly restrict such regulations, by working with lawmakers and one's own grassroots networks.

Activism and lobbying

There are various forms of lobbying and activism, and it is imperative that the Second Amendment activist understands and abides by state and federal lobbying laws. The National Rifle Association, for example, has its own professional state liaisons – their preferred term for lobbyists – while other organizations outright identify their operatives as lobbyists.

There is nothing wrong with lobbying. Every special interest group does it, and this is a way to either help push an agenda, or prevent it from being derailed. In cases where legislatures are stacked against gun rights, thus precluding any probability that meaningful pro-gun legislation could ever pass, it is usually the best and most one can do to prevent stricter gun control bills from being passed.

That hasn't always been the case. Passage of the onerous New York Secure Ammunition and Firearms Enforcement (SAFE) Act of 2013 in response to the Sandy Hook tragedy the previous December – when it didn't even happen in the Empire State but in neighboring Connecticut – was one of those events that sometimes inspires some disappointed activists to scream "sell-out" when nothing is farther from the truth.

Believing that legislatures can be gulled or bullied into submission has proven disastrous on occasion, no matter what the cause or issue. When it comes to gun rights, one will always have allies and opponents, with some people caught in the middle, often by design, so they can use their votes to gain more influence, and vice versa. It is not always a game that can be won.

There is an art to effective lobbying, and not everyone can do it. Lobbyists are registered as such, where private citizens with a special interest are not prohibited from contacting their district legislators and becoming familiar with them and their staffs.

That's where activism comes in. Any citizen can be an activist. It takes passion and knowledge, an ability to keep one's facts straight and no small amount of patience.

'Trophy legislation'

Remember the term "trophy legislation." That's essentially what pet measures pushed by the gun prohibition lobby are, and that brings us around to the so-called "universal background check" campaign that emerged from the gun control push following Sandy Hook. The idea was about the only thing anti-gunners could salvage from their otherwise failed gun control agenda, though the proposal was beaten back in Congress and various state legislatures.

When that didn't work in the Washington State Legislature, an initiative campaign was launched, providing something of a blueprint for subsequent similar efforts in other states, the first of them being Nevada. In other states, the legislative route was tried first, as it was in neighboring Oregon.

In Vermont, a background check measure was signed into law by Gov. Pete Shumlin, though he described it as "a shadow" of the original legislation that would have required checks on all private firearms sales and transfers, with narrow exceptions for immediate family members. That didn't wash in Montpelier, but when the watered-down bill was signed, many Second Amendment activists were still furious.

The final legislation required better reporting of mental health disabilities to the FBI's National Instant Check System (NICS), according to VT Digger, a statewide news service.

While not a "universal background check" as proponents would have liked so as to capture information on every firearm transfer (including loans and gifts) and thus, due to the paperwork involved, create what amounts to a *de facto* gun registry.

When Oregon lawmakers passed that state's new "universal background check" legislation in May 2015, the campaign leading up to the vote essentially included every possible intimation about what the legislation "might help" prevent, without actually claiming anything. The final debate over Senate Bill 941 included all the boilerplate remarks that have become standard fare, as if from a textbook, for such discussions.

The *Portland Oregonian*[3] account included some of the typical assertions one has come to expect from anti-gunners trying to justify adopting legislation that, probably deep in their hearts, they knew would be more symbolic than substance, and have a far greater impact on law-abiding citizens than the criminal element.

"I do not want to take anyone's guns," insisted Corvallis Democrat Rep. Dan Rayfield. "I do not want to register anyone's guns. I want to make the community safer."

The newspaper also quoted Portland Democrat Rep. Jennifer Williamson, one of the bill's chief sponsors, said the final draft included several exemptions to try to ease the burden on legitimate gun owners.

So, she was acknowledging that this new law creates a burden for law-abiding gun owners. Too bad, they'll just have to live with it, while she claimed, "We know that background checks work." In fact, we know that background checks *don't* work to prevent the kinds of incidents that gun control supporters invariably pull out of the hat to sell their latest scheme.

A Republican colleague (notice how these issues always seem to be a division of opinion along party lines?) seemed compelled to point this out. Rep. Mike McLane, the House minority leader, observed, "The tragedies at Sandy Hook, at Clackamas Town Center would not have been stopped by this bill." He was right, but Democrats passed the measure, anyway. More important to have a trophy than to actually do anything meaningful is what the Democrats seemed to be saying with their votes that day.

This is the nature of the legislative gun rights versus gun control debate that has been going on for years. Thanks in part to the financially-enriched vigor being displayed lately by anti-gunners, thanks largely to Bloomberg's Everytown for Gun Safety lobbying organization, gun control fanatics are being supported in their runs for public office, and in their efforts to push the anti-gun agenda.

Anti-gun strategies

The gun prohibition lobby is constantly improving its sales pitch and its delivery, and unless one keeps a constant eye on them, it can be easy for the public to be confused. The National Shooting Sports Foundation (NSSF), a firearms industry trade group, noted in its weekly on-line newsletter Bullet Points 4 that "Anti-gun groups are attempting to bolster their latest push to demonize firearms by trying to equate unintentional (accidental) motor vehicle deaths with firearm-related deaths." Calling it an apples-to-oranges comparison, NSSF pointed readers to reports from the Centers for Disease Control and Prevention and the National Safety Council showing how games are played with data.

"As CDC and NSC report," according to the Bullet Points story, "there were more than 35,000 deaths by unintentional injury in 2013 involving motor vehicles compared to a total of 505 (CDC's number) among all age groups involving firearms. In NSC's Injury Facts 2015 report, firearms are no longer even listed among the top causes of unintentional deaths, which are led by poisoning (more than 38,000 in 2013), motor vehicles, falls, choking, drowning, fire and suffocation. For children under 14, motor vehicle crashes are the leading cause of fatality, with more than 1,401 children dying by this cause in 2011. According to NSC, accidental firearm fatalities declined by 18 percent from 2004 to 2013. Among all these statistics, here is one to keep handy: Firearms are involved in only 0.4 percent of all unintentional fatalities."

But how many state lawmakers read this kind of information before taking a vote on a gun control measure? How is it that this sort of detail seems to escape the public forum?

This omission of information matters greatly when legislators or members of Congress start legislating limits on a constitutionally-guaranteed fundamental civil right. Perhaps some of these politicians simply do not want to know, nor have their colleagues made aware of, such details, instead taking what has become mockingly known as the "Nancy Pelosi approach." This refers to her infamous remark in 2010, during the national debate on the "Affordable Health Care Act," also known as "Obamacare." At the time, she was speaking to the National Association of Counties' legislative conference, as reported at the time by *Politico*. She told the group about the legislation in rather broad terms, and then remarked "But we have to pass the bill so that you can find out what is in it – away from the fog of the controversy."

Pelosi defenders insist she was misunderstood, and the comment has become something of a conservative punch line. In the case of gun control measures, however, the criticism might just fit. These "universal background check" measures have been eyed suspiciously by gun owners, and not without justification. The same thing goes with other gun control legislation.

In Washington State, for example, one almost perennial bill to ban so-called "assault weapons" may have been permanently derailed when it was revealed that buried in the language was a provision that would have allowed police home inspections, without a warrant or probable cause, of the residences of gun owners who had these firearms.

When the *Seattle Times* broke that story in 2013, it interviewed one of the repeat sponsors, an anti-gun Seattle liberal Democrat who insisted that he didn't even know the tenet was in his bill. This fellow was an attorney. The language was quickly removed, but the bill justifiably died in committee.

As the saying goes, the Devil is always in the details.

It falls on the shoulders of firearms group lobbyists and citizen activists to remind lawmakers about this sort of thing, and bring this information to public hearings and other forums. This is why it is imperative for any Second Amendment activist to bring notes to a public hearing, and learn to testify with the kinds of remarks that make good soundbites for television and print reporters.

Public hearings are part of the legislative process, and activists planning to testify should keep their remarks brief, on topic and above all, accurate, and be able to challenge other speakers or even statements from lawmakers, themselves.

For example, earlier we referred to Oregon State Rep. Jennifer Williamson, a backer of that state's gun control measure, who declared that background checks work. That kind of statement can be refuted by offering examples of how guns illegally fall into the wrong hands despite restrictive gun laws. The *New York Daily News* actually provided a textbook case when it reported that the handgun used to murder New York policeman Brian Moore in the spring of 2015.

The newspaper reported that the Taurus revolver had been stolen from a Georgia pawn shop more than three years earlier. There was no background check involved in that theft, and regardless how the handgun wound up in New York City in the hands of a cop killer, a background check law would not have prevented the crime.

Whether the press is willing to report such rebuttals becomes another matter. Op-Ed pieces submitted by Second Amendment advocates could easily point to numerous cases in which the shooter either acquired a firearm illegally, or passed multiple background checks.

Such articles are frequently read by policy makers. That makes it even more important in the legislative arena to be factual and persuasive.

Political theater

Name one thing more predictable than rain in Seattle in November. Theatrics in politics. With the passage of every new gun rights bill in every legislature in the nation, the predictable reaction from anti-gun lawmakers and their control lobby supporters is tantamount to Chicken Little. The sky is always falling.

When Mississippi Gov. Phil Bryant signed legislation making it legal for handguns to be carried in purses, briefcases or other "fully enclosed satchels" without a permit, it was not until after some interesting things were said by opponents who trotted out the tired prediction that people would be given the ability to "act like wild, wild West."

When New York Congressman Chris Collins (R-Twenty-Seventh District) co-sponsored legislation regarding national concealed carry reciprocity, perennial anti-gun Sen. Charles Schumer declared it would be "a nightmare for New York law enforcement." He said there are "20 states you can have a repeated history of mental health police visits and you can get a gun."

His remarks were the core of an anti-gun Op-Ed in the *Buffalo News*, authored by Paul McQuillen, Western New York coordinator for New Yorkers Against Gun Violence. He complained that such legislation "could create life-threatening situations for law enforcement officers."

But then, when did liberals ever really care about police officer safety? That question might best be posed to Milwaukee County, Wisconsin Sheriff David A. Clarke, an African-American lawman who has gained celebrity status among conservatives and gun owners for his willingness to challenge the status quo. He's pro-gun, pro-self-defense and not the least bit shy about throwing down the gauntlet. He has spoken at NRA conventions, and he's been a regular on Fox News.

After the slaying of two Mississippi police officers in the spring of 2015, Sheriff Clarke did something that shocked some people. He blamed, in part, President Barack Obama for – as the *Washington Post* put it – "intentionally weakening police departments by using the Department of Justice."

For many anti-gun politicians, rows of neatly uniformed police officers make good background images for a photo-op when they announce their latest strategy to combat crime by ratcheting down on the rights of law-abiding citizens. These same politicians have a habit of criticizing police for shooting people and otherwise using force, which puts the pols in something of a quandary. While they may envision a world where only cops have guns, they can't quite understand their own hypocrisy about not wanting cops to have guns, either.

As witnessed in Oregon and Washington, where well-financed anti-gun forces were able to pass so-called "universal background checks" against the will of many constituents and vocal county sheriffs, law enforcement only comes in handy when they agree with something, or when they simply stand silently in the background of a speaking politician, as though they did agree. When cops disagree, these politicians don't care to hear.

Clarke's well-timed critique also served another purpose. Gun prohibitionists and their allies in state legislatures and Congress are not above exploiting law enforcement deaths to push their gun control agendas. About the time Clarke went on the warpath against Obama, the FBI released data showing an increase in the number of law enforcement fatalities. That kind of news invariably provides some sort of launch pad for a gun control measure.

Anti-gun irony

Occasionally in politics, especially at the state level, irony steps in to lend gun owners a hand. Such cases sometimes involve outspoken anti-gun lawmakers who wind up on the wrong side in a story involving either the misuse of a firearm or for something like a hunting violation. A rarer occasion would be the discovery of a firearm in somebody's carry-on at an airport security checkpoint, and an embarrassing detention that makes it to the newspapers.

When that happens, it sometimes has a chilling effect on any gun control legislation that just might be waiting in the wings, or already be in play.

The case of Michigan State Sen. Virgil K. Smith is an example. The son of a judge in Detroit, Sen. Smith was arrested and charged with a variety of offenses stemming from an argument with his ex-wife during which Smith allegedly fired several shots into her Mercedes-Benz. Smith was a "D"-rated member of the Michigan legislature before the incident. The incident was widely reported in the *Detroit Free Press.*

However, hypocrisy invariably seems to be a key factor of such cases, where the liberal offender is frequently, if not nearly always, given the benefit of doubt, but a conservative seems to be held to a higher standard.

Former Seattle Police Chief Gil Kerlikowske, during his tenure with that department, had occasionally traveled to the state capitol in Olympia to testify on behalf of gun control measures, in uniform. That came to an abrupt halt after his personally-owned 9mm pistol was stolen from his department car that had been parked on a downtown Seattle street the day after Christmas one year while he and his wife were shopping. The Citizens Committee for the Right to Keep and Bear Arms announced a $1,000 reward for the arrest and conviction of the perpetrator, but the reward has never been paid. That gun is still out there somewhere, and Kerlikowske moved on to higher callings in the Barack Obama administration.

At other times, the anti-Second Amendment crowd has its way regardless, as occurred in Oregon with passage of its "universal background check" legislation, signed into law by Democrat Gov. Kate Brown. The so-called "Oregon Firearms Safety Act" referenced earlier in this chapter was pushed through despite opposition from several county sheriffs and hours of testimony by gun rights activists.

That measure has nothing to do with firearms safety or even crime prevention. As with the similar legislation in Colorado and Washington, the bill seems primarily designed to discourage firearms transfers, loans and sales, while potentially creating *de facto* gun registries, according to critics.

Legislative lessons come hard, and so it is for Second Amendment activists who have far too often sat out elections, failed to contact their local lawmakers or members of Congress, and have generally let others carry their water. That must no longer happen if gun ownership is to be protected and expanded, and

3: CONCEALED CARRY

"Remember the first rule of gunfighting ... have a gun." – Col. Jeff Cooper, founder of the American Pistol Institute

Depending upon one's historical perspective, the carrying of concealed sidearms came about as society became more "civilized" while it was still a matter of habit among many people to carry sidearms for utilitarian and defensive purposes.

In the 19th Century, it was rather common to see people wearing sidearms before and even after the Civil War, and especially west of the Mississippi River, and those who carried concealed handguns were often considered to be scalawags or other lower types given to sneaky and usually illegal behavior. Exceptions to the rule might be gentlemen or ladies who armed themselves with small pistols as a means of protection against those aforementioned scalawags and other lower types.

Pistol permits were used as political tool during New York's Tammany Hall days, but in other jurisdictions the person who felt it necessary to carry a sidearm and do it concealed would get a permit to show that, if he were stopped by the local constable, he was an upstanding citizen and not some criminal who didn't bother with permits.

In many places, particularly the western states, wearing sidearms openly was fairly common well into the

20th Century, and even today one will find people openly armed in many venues, though there may be disagreement as to whether this is being done more as a political statement than for utilitarian purposes.

Permits were also seen by some as a revenue generator and by others as something of a discouragement to the carrying of defensive arms by the general public.

Like it or not, the social pendulum has been swinging back from the disarmament realm to where we are today, with some 13 million citizens licensed to carry and the number is growing constantly. Concealed carry laws have been passed in all 50 states, the last being Illinois, and it took a pair of federal lawsuits by the Second Amendment Foundation (SAF) and National Rifle Association (NRA) to make that happen.

There is nothing fundamentally wrong with being armed. In an age where criminal violence might suddenly unfold in one's immediate proximity, or there might even be some sort of "lone wolf" terrorist attack, the availability of a fighting tool to defend one's self and family or companions is not a luxury but a necessity. In order to "fight crime – shoot back" one must have something with which to shoot.

The concealed carry practitioner is typically someone who wishes to have a gun and keep it out of sight, out of mind, unless the need arises to use it in an emergency. As nationally-recognized firearms and self-defense authority Massad Ayoob has occasionally observed, a gun "is a piece of emergency survival equipment."

Today there are not only scores of handguns designed specifically for defensive concealed carry, but rather large "cottage industries" – if one could even call them that because they have become rather successful businesses – devoted to accessories, from concealment holsters and garments to spare magazine and ammunition pouches, compact handgun grips, personal defense ammunition and even purses and briefcases designed to hold handguns.

Nobody in their right mind leaves the house every morning expecting to be suddenly thrust into a life-or-death situation. On the other hand, nobody leaves home every morning without the expectation that they will return in the evening, at the end of the work day, in good health.

But bad things can happen to good people. As the Boy Scouts taught for generations, always be prepared.

One evening in late April 2015 in Chicago's Logan Square, an Uber driver who just happened to be parked there became the first responder in one of the Windy City's all-too-frequent random shootings, doing something that would have been legally impossible only 24 months previously.

When an irresponsible 22-year-old malcontent opened fire with an illegally-carried handgun, the un-identified 47-year-old hero pulled his own handgun, which was legally licensed and carried, and opened fire. The gun-wielding thug was hit multiple times, with wounds in the shin, knee and lower back.

Authorities in Chicago quickly announced that the Uber driver had acted in self-defense and defense of others, and no charges would be filed. The gunman, however, faced charges of aggravated battery with a firearm and illegal possession of a firearm, according to the local CBS affiliate, which covered the story.

The Second Amendment Foundation, a Washington state-based non-profit that had filed one of the two federal lawsuits, *Moore v. Madigan*, against the State of Illinois to force the legislature to adopt a concealed carry statute, was quick to note in a press release that – had it not been for the legal action – the Uber driver would not have been legally armed and some innocent people could have been seriously hurt.

This shooting, in a city that had once banned handguns until SAF filed its landmark lawsuit that resulted in the 2010 Supreme Court ruling in *McDonald v. City of Chicago*, was said to be ample justification for the legal action. That ruling essentially struck down the Chicago handgun ban and incorporated the Second Amendment to the states. It opened the door to dozens of court challenges against onerous gun laws.

Anecdotal cases like this are used by concealed carry advocates to reinforce their arguments that carrying concealed sidearms for personal protection does contribute to the community welfare. Police officers could not have responded as quickly as the Uber driver, who possibly saved lives by shooting a bad guy.

Concealed means 'concealed!'

Firearms and self-defense instructors will explain that no rational citizen carries a defensive sidearm with the intention to harm or kill another person. They carry in order to keep from being killed by violent criminals or perhaps would-be terrorists looking to get their names on national television. Prior to the San Bernardino attack in December 2015, such people might have been sneered at; now, not so much.

As noted in Chapter One, millions of private citizens are applying for and obtaining concealed carry licenses and permits, and particularly in the aftermath of the California carnage. Anecdotal evidence is all around us and is frequently reported. A typical example came from WJAC News in Pennsylvania, where Centre County Sheriff Denny Nau reported a spike in permit applications during one month in the spring of 2015. He noted that "We see more women and people interested in personal safety. The story also referred to various media reports suggesting a concealed carry increase statewide of 165 percent over the previous decade.

That sort of statistic does not go without notice, and it might inspire even more citizens to exercise their right to carry.

The Second Amendment's reference to "bear arms" means far more than just carrying a firearm around the house. That's the area to which anti-gunners wanted to confine the right to keep and bear arms following the *Heller* ruling in 2008. It was silly, and one might even suggest self-delusional, for gun prohibitionists to contend that a constitutional protection applied only within the walls of one's domicile.

State constitutions have been even more encompassing and expansive than the federal constitution's Second Amendment when it comes to defining the right to keep and bear arms. In Arizona and Washington, for example, the right of the individual citizen to bear arms in defense of himself and the state "shall not be impaired." In both of those states, incidentally, the right to bear arms is recognized to include open carry, but that will be discussed in the next chapter.

Here we talk about concealed carry, the more "popular" approach to going armed in public for one's protection and the defense of his/her family and companions.

First and foremost, "concealed" means *concealed*. The carrying of a firearm in a manner that lends itself to letting others spot a defensive sidearm carried under a cover garment – be it a vest, jacket or loose-fitting, un-tucked shirt – is foolish and offensive, and in some jurisdictions it might even be illegal.

In some states, private businesses can post their premises off limits to firearms, even those legally carried by licensed citizens. Depending upon the state law, such signs might have the force of law, while others are not legally binding, but they do allow for the property owner, say a restaurant owner, summoning police and ordering an armed individual out. If the armed citizen refuses, he could face a charge of criminal trespass.

The best course of action is for the armed citizen to take their business elsewhere.

Places that set themselves up as so-called "gun-free zones" also might be setting themselves up as magnets for criminals. The idea of a "take-over" robbery is hardly unique in America, nor is it a new phenomenon.

Journey back in time to December 1991 when two men described as being armed with "recently stolen pistols" invaded a Shoneys' restaurant in Anniston, Alabama and ordered 20 customers and employees into a walk-in refrigerator. There has been some conjecture that this was planned as a massacre, but nobody will ever know for sure because of the actions of a legally-armed private citizen who was dining at the time and had taken cover under a table.

Thomas Glenn Terry was armed with a .45-caliber semiautomatic pistol. When one of the robbers discovered him, Terry fatally shot the man five times in the torso. His accomplice fired at Terry and slightly wounded him, but the "good guy with a gun" shot that man as well.

This incident was detailed in the *Los Angeles Times* under the headline, "The Massacre We Didn't Hear About." That's because a massacre didn't happen. Instead, two miscreants launched a robbery, and possible massacre plot, and an armed citizen stopped them.

While police seem compelled to caution the public against this sort of armed intervention, the circumstances in Anniston that night precluded any other option. In a split second, one may have to use lethal force in order to save one's self and other innocents. The gun becomes an "emergency survival tool" and the armed citizen becomes the "first responder."

Get reliable information

America, say gun control proponents, is a nation "steeped in the gun culture." Lucky for the Americans, because that culture has given rise to an array of firearms periodicals that have managed to cover virtually all aspects of carrying and using defensive sidearms, or even rifles and shotguns.

Magazine titles such as *American Handgunner, Concealed Carry, Guns & Ammo, Guns, Gun World, Gun Digest, TheGunMag.com* and *American Shooting Journal* appear monthly on magazine racks all over the map. With the advent of the internet, even more on-line publications have sprouted, with all kinds of information – some good, some not so good – under bylines that should leave the reader more than a bit suspicious about the knowledge and qualifications of the authors.

A bit of advice might be timely: On-line essays on blogs that are bylined by nickname only, or by one name, should be considered suspect. Anyone not willing to publish under their proper name shouldn't be taken seriously.

Genuine reliable firearms and self-defense authorities will sign their work and stand by it. Many of these experts have well-established credentials, not only as authors in the magazines, but having written books on the subject. By no small coincidence, most of these individuals are good to exceptional marksmen and women. Some of them are serious shooting competitors and others have backgrounds in law enforcement, private security or a combination of experience that has involved pulling a trigger.

These experts are invariably staunch Second Amendment practitioners (as opposed to "supporters") who understand from years of experience that sometimes well-intentioned people do foolish things. They've devoted their professional lives to helping prevent that sort of thing and instead offer instruction and insight where it matters.

The aforementioned magazines are loaded with product reviews on new guns and ammunition, accessories and sometimes advice.

To say that America is "steeped in the gun culture" is not insulting to those citizens who have assumed responsibility for their own safety. That "culture" may just give these people a winning edge over the criminal element.

Don't overlook good books on the subject of armed self-defense. Possibly the most famous of these is *In the Gravest Extreme: The Role of the Firearm in Personal Protection* by the aforementioned Massad F. Ayoob. His follow-up volume, *Deadly Force: Understanding Your Right to Self Defense*, is also considered "must" reading by many instructors.

Ayoob also authored the *Gun Digest Book of Concealed Carry*, but he is not the only resource for such information. One will find any number of educational and enlightening books on the subject by reputable authors.

Take a quiz

If you are one of the millions of legally armed citizens, take this little quiz:

How many times a week do you carry your defensive firearm away from home?

What kind of gun is it? What caliber, make and model?

How do you carry that sidearm? In a pocket, purse or a holster?

Is that a shoulder holster, belt holster, "inside-the-waistband" (IWB), ankle or pocket holster?

How often do you practice at the range with your defensive sidearm?

How often do you clean your defensive sidearm?

• Do you socialize with other gun owners, and participate in shooting leagues?

• Have you taken an advanced self-defense course from such places as Thunder Ranch, Gunsite Academy, Firearms Academy of Seattle or one of the other reputable "shooting schools?"

• Do you know where your defensive sidearm is right now, and in what condition (unloaded, loaded, loaded with round in chamber)?

• Where do you store your firearm(s) when not in use?

These are the kinds of things that prudent armed citizens should be able to answer, almost without thinking about it. Notice, the quiz did not include the kind of nonsense one often encounters on internet gun forums in which there are endless debates about how many spare magazines one should carry when grocery shopping, and whether one has a back-up gun.

Some people refer to participants in such conversations as "mall ninjas." It's easy to identify these individuals. They wear cargo pants, "tactical" belts, "tactical vests" and carry "tactical knives" and "tactical flashlights" while carrying their guns in "tactical holsters." If underwear was "tactical," they'd be wearing it.

They might as well instead be wearing a neon sign that says "Hi, I'm carrying a gun."

The more inconspicuous one can be while armed, the better. You don't want to stand out in a crowd; you want to disappear into it. If something really bad happens in your immediate proximity, being the first person shot because the bad guy identified you as a potential challenger is not the way you want to be remembered.

The right to carry should not be confused with the ability to be stupid in public. Your conduct reflects on every other armed citizen, like it or not. Watch your behavior, take care with your wardrobe, don't deliberately telegraph that you are carrying a defensive firearm and use your better judgment to avoid places and situations that simply reek of trouble waiting to happen.

And there are times when an armed citizen suddenly finds himself/herself in the middle of a deadly situation in which it is better to not open fire. One man who found himself thrust into such an event was Joseph Zamudio, the armed citizen who helped tackle

Tucson gunman Jared Lee Loughner after he opened fire, wounding former Congresswoman Gabrielle Giffords and killing six other people.

Dr. John R. Lott Jr, founder and head of the Crime Prevention Research Center (CPRC), wrote about Zamudio, who was carrying a 9mm semiautomatic pistol that day and didn't use it, in a *New York Times* opinion piece.

"But Joe showed that law-abiding citizens with concealed handguns can exercise excellent judgment in when is the right time to use their guns," Lott observed. "When it made more sense for him to tackle the attacker, he did that rather than use his gun. Everything from public school shootings to church shootings has been stopped by citizens with concealed handguns."

Lott said something else in that short essay that bears repeating.

"Just as you can deter criminals with higher arrest or conviction rates," Lott observed, "letting victims defend themselves also deters criminals. With concealed handguns, criminals don't know whether victim can defend themselves until they attack. More people legally carrying a concealed handgun means that someone can get to the crime scene faster."

As we have previously noted, the legally-armed citizen might become the "first responder" in an incident. Thus, it can pay off to practice, and that can involve many different endeavors that go well beyond simply shooting stationary paper targets.

Countless numbers of licensed concealed carriers have participated in additional training courses, and many more take their shooting skills seriously enough to visit a gun range at least once or twice a month. Many commercial ranges have shooting leagues and additional class offerings on such things as lethal force and the law, or firearms retention.

There are also competitions that can test one's skills. Shooting competitions sharpen one's motor and marksmanship skills while advanced courses sharpen one's mind about when, and when *not*, to shoot.

Demonizing armed citizens

Gun prohibitionists are never shy about finding ways to condemn and demonize legally-armed citizens. When the Ohio Legislature adopted a concealed carry blanket recognition that enables licensed citizens from other states to carry in the Buckeye State, anti-gun-rights advocates were vocally opposed.

The *Columbus Dispatch* quoted Jennifer Thorne, executive director of the Ohio Coalition Against Gun Violence. She contended that the 2015-enacted law contained "a number of troubling provisions."

"There's nothing for us to celebrate in this bill," she said, and then she added a remark that seems to have become part of the fabric of the anti-self-defense movement.

"Everyone who is carrying a gun is a good guy up until the moment they aren't," she asserted.

Likewise, the story also quoted Laura Cutilletta, a staff attorney for the San Francisco-based Law Center to Prevent Gun Violence. Expressing ardent opposition to concealed carry reciprocity, she told the newspaper, "Our main concern is with the reciprocity part of it. That is exposing everyone in Ohio to a dangerous situation."

What Thorne and Cutilletta did was create an impression — or at least attempt to — that citizens who are legally-armed are dangerous people waiting for an opportunity to cause mayhem.

Indeed, one gun prohibition group, the Violence Prevention Center, has issued a report called "Concealed Carry Killers." As noted by Townhall.com, Lott took this group to task over what many consider to be "flawed" reporting, using data from a single state to question the VPC's hypothesis about concealed carriers being potential criminals.

Writing in the National Review, Lott called the VPC's assertions about concealed carry permit holders "bogus." Lott did some checking and concluded that VPC was essentially cooking the data, asserting that the group includes "legitimate self-defense cases in which no charges were filed or the permit holder was charged and later exonerated" in its reports.

"Assume, for the sake of argument," Lott wrote, "that the Violence Policy Center's claim that concealed-handgun permits were responsible for 636 deaths in seven years (May 2007-March 2014) is correct. One has to note that there are over 11 million concealed-handgun permits in the U.S. right now. With an annual number of deaths of 90, that means 0.00083 percent of concealed-carry permit holders were responsible for a shooting death each year. Removing suicides from the total reduces the rate even more, to 0.00058 percent.

"The conjuring up of bogus numbers like these," he asserted, "has become a mainstay of gun-control groups. That also includes the 'studies' financed by Michael Bloomberg's millions. However, a group of researchers, of whom I am one, are setting up the Crime Prevention Research Center to uncover and counter these misleading claims."

As noted earlier, Dr. Lott did launch the CPRC, and this group has continued probing the relationship between firearms and violent crime, while challenging some notions that had been accepted as fact.

Unfortunately, gun control proponents only read what they want, understanding and interpreting it the way they want, and evidence to the contrary against their notions about armed private citizens be damned.

Take the case of anti-gun Washington State Sen. Jeannie Darnielle who remarked during a public hearing on a proposed background check bill in early 2014, "I am not a person who handles guns. I don't own guns. I don't…they shock me, quite frankly. We're an open carry state and when I see people open carrying their guns, while it may be perfectly legal, it creates a visceral, personal, physical reaction in me as it does in other people…"

Sen. Darneille's remarks illustrated what gun rights activists are actually up against nationwide; an emotion toward firearms in some people that approaches revulsion. Despite all facts and logic to the contrary, opponents of private firearms ownership, and especially opponents of concealed or open carry (a subject to be discussed in the next chapter), one cannot convince such people that the overwhelming majority of legally-armed citizens are responsible members of their communities.

'The best means…'

Fortunately, not all state lawmakers are like Sen. Darnielle. Indiana State Rep. Jim Lucas is an example of the other side of the argument, and he made a compelling one in the pages of the *Indianapolis Star*. In a 353-

word letter, Rep. Lucas noted his efforts to "eliminate licensing requirements for innocent people to carry a firearm." He added that, "a firearm is still the best means of defending one's self and loved ones against those that have no regard for human life or laws."

Lucas also alluded to the proposed "Concealed Carry Reciprocity Act (S.498)" that had been introduced by U.S. Sen. John Cornyn, (R-Texas). This legislation would eliminate a state's ability to infringe upon constitutionally protected gun rights of individuals from another state who can carry guns within its own borders. It's an idea that alarms and infuriates gun control proponents at the same time, and they cranked up the volume on their opposition almost immediately.

"Once again," Lucas observed, "we are hearing the same tired rhetoric from those who wish to infringe upon, and even take away, the gun rights of innocent men and women. Applications for concealed carry permits in Indiana continue to explode as hundreds of thousands of Hoosier men and women realize that they are the first line of defense in protecting themselves and loved ones."

Whether Congress would ever pass a national reciprocity/recognition statute that requires all the states merely to recognize all other states' concealed carry licenses may become less important over time than the discussion that such proposals invariably ignites.

Unfortunately, some Second Amendment activists have been consistently opposed to such legislation on the theory that it would allow Congress to set concealed carry standards nationwide. However, that is not really the case, same as Congress has not set some national standard of driving. Each state's carry laws – at least under some of the national reciprocity proposals

– would remain intact. It would be up to the individual licensed citizen to study up on the laws of any state in which he or she would be traveling armed, and abide by those regulations while in that jurisdiction. "When in Rome," as the saying goes, "do as the Romans do."

This is where the resources of the Traveler's Guide and Handgunlaw.us would prove themselves indispensable. It might also be prudent to find any of the numerous local books that detail individual state gun laws. There are several available, from different authors.

Element of surprise

Are there advantages to carrying concealed over openly-carrying a defensive firearm? Many will argue that there are, and the chief reason among them is the element of surprise. Earlier in this chapter, we mentioned the case out of Anniston, Alabama in which a legally-armed restaurant patron turned the tables on a pair of armed robbers.

There are lots of stories like that, and the one thing they all seem to have in common is that the criminals were taken completely by surprise. Occasionally, such outlaws are stopped literally dead in their tracks.

Take the case of the Houston man who was just opening up one morning at a business in East Houston, Texas. That unidentified armed citizen suddenly found himself at gunpoint from a would-be robber who demanded the bag under his arm, apparently believing it contained cash, according to an account from KTRK, the local ABC affiliate.

The store employee did not have money in the bag, but at this point, it seems possible that the robber may have intended to shoot him regardless.

With a gun at his head, the store employee drew his own legally-carried handgun and fired four shots at almost point blank range. All but one of those rounds apparently connected and the gunman fell with bullet wounds to the chest. He died later at a local hospital, and his intended victim was not injured.

A concealed carry license is not a hunting license, and they are not designed to provide armed citizens any justification for intervening in a crime. They are designed to provide citizens with a defensive tool to prevent becoming a statistic.

Tens of thousands, if not hundreds of thousands, of professional people operating their businesses keep guns handy. This is especially true in the pharmacy field as a defense against drug store robbers. A pharmacist in Pinch, West Virginia is one such individual. According to WCHS News, a would-be robber tried a mid-morning stick-up at a pharmacy in the community, only to have his career cut permanently short by the armed pharmacist.

When the gunman entered the store and aimed a firearm at store staff, the pharmacist drew his own gun, according to the report, and shot the man fatally.

What is perhaps refreshing to many in the firearms community is that a number of law enforcement professionals have stopped advising people to submit and then call them police. One such example was Lauderdale County, Mississippi Sheriff Billy Sollie, quoted by WTOK following an armed robbery gone-bad in his jurisdiction.

"It's becoming more and more commonplace where citizens are arming themselves and telling the bad guys, 'Don't mess with me,'" the sheriff stated.

Sheriff Sollie's comments were underscored when the Florida Department of Agriculture and Consumer Services reported that in May 2015 it reached a milestone of 1.4 million active concealed weapons licenses. That figure represented a jump of more than 100,000 licenses from the previous year, and there was no indication that the demand was tapering off.

Indeed, the report noted, the Sunshine State had passed a law allowing license applications to be left at the offices of tax collectors in at least ten counties.

Likewise, in Missouri, the *St. Louis Post-Dispatch* reported that concealed carry permit applications were way up and that was leading to an unintended consequence: Gun thefts from automobiles. The story noted that many people were losing their firearms to car prowlers who know that people cannot carry firearms into so-called "gun-free zones" such as Busch Stadium.

St. Louis Police Chief Sam Dotson told the newspaper that "criminals have this figured out."

This brings up another concern for the legally-armed citizen: Do you have a lock box in your vehicle for such occasions when you cannot carry your defensive sidearm into a restaurant, private business, sports stadium or government building?

Back in 2013, then-Seattle Mayor Mike McGinn, in what many saw as a re-election bid to appeal to his far-Left base, initiated a "Gun-Free Business" program with the help of the local gun control organization, Washington CeaseFire. McGinn lost his re-election bid to an even farther-Left challenger, State Sen. Ed

Murray, who continued supporting the program. More than 100 businesses quickly signed up, but one thing that was overlooked at the time was that some of these establishments were already off-limits to firearms.

Sarcastically dubbed "Zones of Happy Thoughts" by critics, these gun-free businesses were essentially practicing social bigotry against legally-armed citizens, but to Seattle liberals, that didn't seem to matter. Indeed, this sort of prejudicial treatment is encouraged by anti-gun-rights liberals.

Seattle's two sports stadiums are located within a one-block distance of one another – Century Link Field (Seattle Seahawks) and Safeco Field (Seattle Mariners) – and they also prohibit firearms, even though they were built with public funds. King County danced around the state preemption statute by hiring private companies to manage both facilities, and a stipulation in the contracts was a gun ban.

Unlike the St. Louis experience, Seattle police told the authors that over the course of several years, there had not been any indications that firearms were being stolen out of cars parked by sports fans attending games in the Jet City. Both cities have large parking garages near the respective stadiums, so there is really no difference in terms of automobile security.

Criminals have plans, too

There is an often-used adage that many old soldiers have used that pretty much spells out the sudden and violent nature – as well as the uncertainty of the outcome – of a gunfight. "The plan goes out the window when the first shot is fired in anger."

There are countless firearms forums on the Internet that deal with defensive firearms, concealed and open carry, self-defense issues and firearms in general. Participants often reveal how they have "a plan" in the event this or that happens, be the scenario in a restaurant, supermarket, at home, on vacation, whatever. Alas, for the average citizen, one key component is invariably missing. The criminal did not participate in formulating the plan, and they've got more moves, more tricks and more strategies than their intended victims. After all, they do crime for a living.

The other side to that story is the surprise that comes to these villains when their intended victim happens to pull out a gun, rather than a wallet, and opens fire. Many a miscreant has met an untimely end, or had his career interrupted by such an unexpected reaction.

That's about how things fell apart for a couple of armed robbers who tried to hold up a business called Kricks Corner in Reading, Pennsylvania in November 2013. As the two bandits emerged from the business with stolen money, lottery tickets and cigarettes, an armed private citizen confronted the masked pair, told them he was calling the police, and advised them to stay put.

That's when everything suddenly went to hell. According to WFMZ News, the bad guys drew their guns, presumably thinking they had the drop on this Good Samaritan. But the good guy had a gun and he fatally shot both William Medina and Robert De Carr. A third man, who was reportedly driving the getaway car, was subsequently arrested.

In the aftermath came protestations from the families of the dead men, as is often the case. Medina's mother, quoted by WFMZ, complained that her son's death was "not fair."

"(William) had no right to lose his life over something that man could have called the police for," Medina told the reporter. "He took the law into his own hands and walked away scot-free."

Nobody has a "right" to be shot dead during the commission of an armed robbery. That's just their bad luck in some cases. That the armed citizen was not prosecuted should not be a signal to other armed citizens that they will experience the same outcome if they intervene in a felony crime, or just happen to stumble into it. In this specific case, police said the armed citizen acted within the law.

There's a moral that almost invariably escapes the families of people killed in the commission of crimes. If the decedents hadn't been engaged in some criminal activity, they would not be dead.

That knowledge often comes as little solace to the armed citizen who acts legally in defense of himself/herself or others. Those who carry defensive sidearms, and have had to use them, may experience a wide range of emotions, from elation at being alive to a strange sense of guilt at having taken a human life, or in this case, multiple lives.

People say with every right comes responsibility. So it is with the right to carry. But there's something else that comes along with carrying a firearm for personal protection, and that is remorse.

Yet, in order to feel remorse, one must be alive. When one is the dead victim of a violent criminal, one feels nothing at all.

4: OPEN CARRY

"Contrary to the concerns of some opponents of open carry, such measures have not led to wild-West shootouts or other serious consequences."—Tulsa World editorial, 2-25-2012

Open carry is a prickly subject for a lot of people, and it became even moreso in mid-2015 when Texas Gov. Greg Abbott signed into law a statute that made the open carry of sidearms in public – provided one had a concealed handgun license – legal in the Lone Star State.

It was a fairly bold move for the Texas governor, and it brought the normal wails from anti-gunners who predicted that it was a prelude to everything from increased urban violence to the sky falling. But it also established Abbott as a man who kept his word. He had promised to sign an open carry bill it if landed on his desk, and he did.

The fact that open carry is legal in many states has enabled a relative small number of attention-grabbers to engage in provocative behavior that, many argue – including some serious open carry activists – has done more harm than good for the movement. And it is a movement within the larger firearms community, make no mistake about that.

Thousands of law-abiding private citizens carry sidearms openly as part of their daily routines, for any number of reasons, or for no reason at all. One doesn't need a reason to exercise a civil right, whether out in the open or covered up, but one should be ever cognizant of the fact that bad behavior while visibly armed can be monumentally foolish if the intention is to further the cause of open carry.

Indeed, there are open carry advocates in every state, and they even have their own website, Open Carry. org (OCDO), founded some years ago by two Second Amendment activists. The practice has spread as increasing numbers of people have discovered that it is legal in their jurisdiction, and leaders in the movement do not look kindly on the foolish.

There is a new consideration, however, because of the potential for "lone wolf" terrorist actions. Like it or not, an open carrier could become the first casualty as noted earlier.

When legalized open carry was being considered by the Oklahoma legislature, the *Tulsa World* editorialized in something of a voice of resignation that the measure would become law, and the state needed to make sure it was a responsible, rational statute. The newspaper's editorial board seemed genuinely impressed that, "a surprising number of states even allow open carry of handguns without a license. Contrary to the concerns of some opponents of open carry, such measures have not led to wild-West shootouts or other serious consequences."

For a newspaper to write such a candid editorial on a subject that often elicits both fury and fear simultaneously among gun control advocates takes a lot. And when the editorial added some favorable arguments for open carry, it made anti-gunners cringe.

"There are some arguments for open carry," the newspaper reasoned. "It is easier to draw a weapon that isn't concealed. And it's probably accurate that criminals will not open carry because they don't want to draw attention to themselves. Would law-abiding residents who openly carry a weapon serve as a deterrent to crime? Maybe, in a limited number of incidents."

While that assessment may not delight some hardcore open carry advocates, others find it refreshing from any mainstream news organ.

Why should anyone carry openly when it may be far less socially offensive to carry concealed, if one must carry a firearm at all? What's the benefit of potentially creating more enemies of armed citizenship?

Those are fair questions.

Open Carry advocates will argue that it serves as a deterrent to crime. The sight of someone carrying a revolver or semi-auto pistol on his or her hip can have a chilling effect on many criminals who don't want to end their careers abruptly by being shot.

There have been cases involving open carriers who did intervene in emergency situations and actually shoot a criminal perpetrator.

Some of the open carry purists refuse to carry concealed, arguing that they have a right to carry a firearm under the federal constitution and many state constitutions that protect the right "to bear" arms. They insist that walking peaceably down a street or into a private business should be no cause for alarm because they're not doing anything wrong.

But it can be offensive to some people. That's where open carry activists occasionally put themselves into the position of being a teacher and an ambassador for the practice.

Writing in the *Yale Law Journal*, Jonathan Meltzer shared an observation in an article headlined "Open

Carry for All: Heller and Our Nineteenth Century Second Amendment" that perhaps best explains the dilemma open carriers face.

"Opponents see open carry as the worst of the pro-gun movement—a practice aimed more at provocation and showmanship than at any legitimate safety goal," he explained with footnotes. "Meanwhile, many proponents of gun rights recognize how unusual and fear-inducing open carry is in many situations, and how much many Americans prefer to carry weapons concealed. They worry that a constitutional right limited to open carry would prevent many law-abiding citizens from carrying weapons due to the stigma of carrying openly. Still, even if this result is impractical and unpopular, it is the most loyal reading of *Heller*. And because the Court has committed to an originalist methodology for the Second Amendment, complaints about open carry's lack of agreement with modern practice ought to have very little sway."

True enough, opponents of open carry despise the practice and are alarmed by it; so much so, that they will try to spread their personal paranoia to the masses, by encouraging boycotts of businesses that allow open carry on their premises, to lobbying lawmakers to outlaw the practice.

Some open carriers are their own worst enemies, particularly when it comes to striking poses with long guns inside different business establishments; images that subsequently are spread across the Internet on sites such as Facebook. This sort of behavior is not the best image one could put forward.

If one wishes to make a political statement, rent a billboard or take out an advertisement in the local newspaper.

Most open carriers stick with handguns that are neither obtrusive nor provocative. Carried in a belt holster, a sidearm is often not even noticed. Going about one's business with a holstered pistol on one's belt can often draw little or no attention, which many in the open carry movement contend is their goal. They want open carry to be accepted as a normal behavior, by normal citizens. In other words: Show-offs need not apply.

'It's not illegal, even if alarming'

All of that said, there is no indication that open carry practitioners have created any kind of public nuisance, nor do they present a *danger* to the public, notwithstanding any emotional discomfort that some people have allegedly felt. Indeed, in some cases, it is the open carrier who faces victimization at the hands of irrational people who take extreme measures.

One such case unfolded in Yakima, Washington that made headlines far beyond the boundaries of that east-central Washington community, located in the Yakima Valley about 150 miles southeast from Seattle.

An armed citizen named Brandon Walker was shopping at a Wal-Mart with three of his children when he was accosted by a man named Trevor Zumwalt, according to the *Yakima Herald*. This was no ordinary incident, because, according to several published reports, Zumwalt grabbed a metal baseball bat from a display and attempted to strike Walker on the head. Instead, he hit Walker on the shoulder.

Walker was openly carrying a .357-caliber Sig Sauer pistol because it was warm out that day. Open carry is legal in the Evergreen State and has even been affirmed by state appellate courts, and eastern Washington might be called "gun country," as opposed to the Seattle area. Politics and lifestyles contrast sharply between the two regions.

Making the incident even more bizarre was the fact that the suspect was a rather short fellow, while Walker – the man who was attacked – stands just over six feet tall and weighed 360 pounds at the time, according to news coverage of the incident.

Yet a metal bat can be a lethal weapon, and Walker drew his pistol and ordered his assailant to the floor. Walker held him there until police arrived and carted him off to jail.

It was never quite clear why Walker was attacked, whether it was an attack grounded in some anti-gun philosophy, or perhaps the suspect was attempting to seize Walker's handgun. Only Walker's self-control saved the suspect, who could have been justifiably shot in self-defense, since he had apparently turned a bat into a lethal weapon.

Instead, Walker ordered Zumwalt to the floor and held him there until police arrived. Zumwalt was charged with a felony. Walker wasn't charged with anything.

No right to not be offended

In states that have constitutional protections for the right to bear arms, anti-gunners have an interesting dilemma if they try pushing for a ban on open carry. Since the right to bear arms should prevent a state from banning all forms of carry, if open carry is somehow legislatively prohibited, then there is a rational argument that the state would henceforth have to allow concealed carry without a permit.

So far, it has not come to that, and one gets the sense that gun prohibitionists have not thought that far ahead on the unintended consequences of instituting such a ban. A court challenge would almost certainly follow.

In what perhaps might be as good a statement as one might find on open carry, the Washington State Court of Appeals observed in an unpublished ruling in the case of *State v. Gregory Elijah Casad* that open carry is legal, even if alarming to some people.

Casad had been arrested in the city of Port Angeles carrying two rifles wrapped in what appeared to be a towel. While Casad was a convicted felon – a fact that the original complainant could not have known, and neither did the police officers when they responded – the court found that the police had no authority to detain him for merely walking down the street with the firearms. He was actually taking the two rifles to a nearby pawn shop.

"We note," the court said, "that, in connection with this case, several individuals have commented that they would find it strange, maybe shocking, to see a man carrying a gun down the street in broad daylight. Casad's appellate counsel conceded that she would personally react with shock, but she emphasized that an individual's lack of comfort with firearms does not equate to reasonable alarm. We agree. It is not unlawful for a person to responsibly walk down the street with a visible firearm, even if this action would shock some people."

Forget the specifics of the Casad case and focus instead on what the court said about "an individual's lack of comfort with firearms does not equate to reasonable alarm," and how it is legal for a person to walk down a street with a visible firearm." There is no right to not be offended or alarmed. There is a right to bear arms.

Many open carry activists have a good understanding of the law, though at times some people can be rather annoying when they start trying to tell police officers about the law. Some years ago in Washington State, an open carry activist went to considerable effort to educate local police agencies and some county sheriff's departments about open carry, which is not delineated anywhere in Washington statute, but is protected by a series of court rulings dating back nearly a century. In some cases, the agencies even added refreshers and training bulletins on the subject to all of their officers.

Different states handle the practice differently. It should not be surprising that in more rural areas, county sheriffs and small-town police departments have a far different perspective on open carry than do the administrations of large metropolitan agencies. Indeed, in some states – Arizona, Idaho and Montana, for example – it is not unusual to find people openly carrying sidearms. There is no history of such people harming anyone.

Looking back momentarily at Texas, where Gov. Abbott signed legislation allowing the practice – which had been outlawed since the post-Civil War era – is perhaps more of a signal that the nation is dividing into two camps philosophically.

Abbott even went the extra mile, signing the legislation at an indoor gun range. That was no political misstep; Abbott knew exactly the kind of message that would send. In a statement at the signing, he noted,

"There is nothing more important in democracy than the voice of the people stepping up and saying 'We expect the Constitution of the United States of America to be our guiding doctrine'."

At the time he also thanked the National Rifle Association and Texas State Rifle Association, further poking the gun prohibition lobby, which had strenuously opposed the legislation.

An election mattered

Not everyone agrees about open carry, and whether it is legal and what kinds of limitations may be placed upon people who do it. What happened in Arkansas provides an important lesson on why elections matter, and why sometimes even good ideas come across imperfectly when they are hammered into the form of legislation.

When Act 746 was passed back in 2013, there was disagreement whether the new law allowed the open carry of firearms in a peaceable manner. At the time, then-Attorney General Dustin McDaniel opined that the law did not allow open carry. That didn't stop some people from doing it without a problem. The *Arkansas Democrat-Gazette* online reported on one man with an activist group who had carried for two years without an incident.

In 2014, a new attorney general was elected, Republican Leslie Rutledge. The following spring, three state lawmakers sought an updated opinion from her office. This was after she had already indicated, according to the newspaper account, that the law does allow a person to carry a firearm "if he or she did so without the intent to unlawfully employ it against another person."

About the same time, the police chief in Rogers issued a statement on open carry on the department's Facebook page that simply noted the department "will not make arrests on individuals who are simply openly carrying a firearm.

"However," the statement continued, "we will respond to calls for service of armed individuals for further investigation to determine they are acting within the law. As we have previously stated, there is no textbook definition of what a 'bad guy' looks like. The only way to determine if someone is legally carrying a firearm, or if they have some other intent, is to talk to them.

'"We ask for the cooperation of those individuals who choose to openly carry firearms and to assist our officers in doing their jobs with the least amount of disruption of everyone's time," the statement concluded.

If a law is not clear about its parameters, it usually winds up being challenged in court.

The *Democrat-Gazette's* coverage of the issue was very detailed and touched a lot of bases, quoting lawmakers, law enforcement and a county prosecutor. The latter, Benton County Prosecutor Nathan Smith told the newspaper that open carry by itself is not a prosecutable offence, but carrying a weapon for other purposes can be.

The newspaper also noted that in Arkansas, there are between 8,000 and 10,000 members of a group calling itself the Patriots of Act 746, and that between the law's passage in 2013 and spring of 2015, four of them had been arrested for open carrying, and three had been found not guilty in court.

Wherever open carry is practiced, it could get the attention of police who will be responding to "man with a gun" calls. That's something noted by Arkansas Carry, and only education and time will address this.

In the meantime, we will no doubt continue reading about situations like the one in Grand Rapids, Michigan as reported by the *Detroit Free Press* and other outlets. This particular case involved a man named Johann Deffert, described as an "open carry gun advocate," who was reportedly wearing camouflage, singing to himself and carrying what the newspaper called "a loaded assault pistol strapped to his leg" in front of a church.

Someone called the police, who responded, disarmed him and briefly put him in handcuffs while sorting it all out.

Deffert sued, contending that his constitutional rights had been violated, but federal Judge Janet Neff at the U.S. District Court threw his case out. The police, she said, had responded to a 911 call about a man with a gun. Michigan law allows for open carry, and as the newspaper described the situation, "police agencies around Michigan are grappling with increasingly contentious clashes with gun advocates who are showing up at places like churches, schools and government complexes armed with assault rifles and handguns, part of their campaign to educate residents on gun laws, and desensitize the public to the sight of guns."

The case was discussed at some length by Michigan members of OCDO, and they were an unhappy lot. As one summed it up: "Lesson here: Don't sing and carry at the same time. I can see this leading to a flurry of frantic 911 calls anytime an OCer is spotted."

There appears to be much to that. People who regularly open carry without problems will explain that they behave as they would if carrying concealed or not carrying at all. Translation: They're not doing anything that would call attention to themselves. They're minding their own business. There are some others, however, who cannot seem to go outside without attracting attention.

Whether one agrees or disagrees, open carry is legal and constitutionally-protected, but that's not *carte blanche* to engage in behavior that may unnecessarily raise alarms among others or bring unnecessary attention.

This was an observation from a police group official quoted by the *Free Press* story: "We're seeing sporadic reports of it from around the state, those who are trying to draw attention to themselves and it's needlessly alarming people. People aren't used to seeing someone brandish a gun in front of their kids' schools." In that, Robert Stevenson, executive director of the 1,100-member Michigan Association of Chiefs of Police has a point.

The newspaper account of Deffert's case also mentioned another case from Michigan's Oakland County involving a man who "posted a video of himself, walking armed with a pistol, on the Oakland County complex in Pontiac, where he was videotaping a lot where sheriff's office employees park."

According to the story, when he was approached by some deputies "including one who appeared to snatch a piece of identification from Nixon — he became angry and began to curse at the deputies before leaving." Now, what's that all about?

A third incident discussed in the same story came from Sterling Heights, where two men were detained near the Henry Ford Medical Center. Both were carrying rifles and handguns, they were disarmed, handcuffed and held for about ten minutes. Police then gave them back their firearms, and they subsequently sued, arguing that their constitutional rights had been violated.

Again, the newspaper said, the court ruled otherwise.

U.S. District Judge Robert Cleland put it rather bluntly in his decision, quoted by the newspaper: "The single reasonable conclusion is that plaintiffs were knowingly acting in a provocative manner hoping to foment an interaction and cause a disturbance. As events show, they succeeded nicely."

Trouble in paradise

Open Carry has also been to court in Florida, where state statute prohibits the practice, and a challenge to that law failed in early 2015. In the spring of 2015, an appeals court panel upheld the Sunshine State's law preventing open carry, based on a 2012 case involving the arrest of a man in Fort Pierce for carrying a sidearm openly.

The three-judge panel, as reported by the News Service of Florida, said that "Florida's requirements to obtain a permit for concealed carry are not so burdensome, or so onerous, as to make the ability to obtain a permit illusory." Naturally, activists disagreed, and promised to push for a revision in the state law.

But there was some good news in the ruling for all gun owners. Attorney Eric Friday, who represented the defendant in this case, recognized that the court did say that there is a right to carry a gun outside the home for personal protection.

Activism paid off

While there is enough anecdotal evidence of silly behavior by some people while open carrying that can be watched online thanks to YouTube, there is little said about the responsible people who openly carry sidearms on a daily basis and never experience a problem. Others, it seems, can't venture too far from their own front doors before they've got trouble. Go figure.

The difference, of course, is that people who don't find themselves in trouble don't wind up on YouTube, perhaps because they never intended to be there in the first place. People who go about their business open carrying without benefit of some companion with a video recording device at the ready don't attract attention.

Some years ago, Gray Peterson, an open carry activist in Washington State, spent countless hours researching that state's statutes and legal documents, and the result was a one-man education effort aimed at local police agencies, both sheriff's departments and municipal police departments. His efforts were not wasted, as he met with some agencies, and traded e-mail or phone calls with others and in many cases, the departments issued training bulletins to their officers about open carry.

In an e-mail, he recalled to the authors that he had been interested in firearms for self-defense since his teens in Florida, and eventually got a license in Oregon when he was 21. The Arizona native knew that Washington's constitutional right-to-bear-arms provision was identical to his state's, but the two states regulate firearms a bit differently.

His initial research spanned seven months and he had some help from a friend. Peterson's first foray at contacting a police agency was in Federal Way, and once that agency produced a training bulletin, he took that to other departments.

"That basically changed the ballgame," he said.

Ironically, a case called *State v. Randolph Spencer* involving a Federal Way man who was prosecuted for openly carrying a rifle is part of the fabric of the open carry movement in Washington State. In that case, the court of appeals ruled that there was really no problem with Spencer's carrying of a loaded pistol, for which he was licensed to carry concealed, but the rifle – identified as an AK – with a loaded magazine carried openly was enough to trigger the state statute about warranting alarm in another person.

An effort like Peterson's can be far more productive than two guys walking around with long guns and video recorders, and a belligerent attitude, looking for a confrontation. That sort of antic can backfire, which we will discuss at greater length in a later chapter.

For an activist to almost single-handedly provide an educational opportunity to several law enforcement agencies and actually turn many of them around on open carry rights is no small achievement, and it wins friends rather than creates critics.

Indeed, in one case dealing with one of the larger sheriff's departments in the Evergreen State, one activist taking advantage of Peterson's groundwork actually helped the agency write its training bulletin, which still is available and in use today.

A matter of opinion

One interesting anecdote about open carry was how a statute adopted in 2013 in Arkansas was defined by a former attorney general – a Democrat – and the Republican who replaced him in 2014. As KFSM News reported, former AG Dustin McDaniel said open carry of handguns was illegal under Act 746. But when his replacement, Republican Leslie Rutledge, was quizzed about whether the law allows open carry as part of a news story in mid-2015, her response was quite the opposite.

Rutledge was not alone. Arkansas Gov. Asa Hutchinson also told the station that, in his opinion, open carry is legal so long as there is no criminal intent. The same opinion was voiced by Lt. Gov. Tim Griffin.

Here, again, is another example of what appears to be a difference in political philosophy, with a Democrat coming down on one side and a Republican on the other when they interpret a specific law regarding gun rights. This is not always a hard-and-fast rule, but more often than not, Democrats seem to favor more restrictive gun laws, and more narrow interpretations of existing statutes, than Republicans. Over the years, Democrats have come to be known as "The party of gun control" for a reason.

In Arkansas as elsewhere, open carry activists can sometimes be their own worst enemies, but when there is a high-profile disagreement about the meaning of a law, it throws the debate into a proverbial "cocked hat." And this is where politics takes over.

Entering into the fray were county sheriffs who also announced they would not be arresting anyone for openly carrying sidearms.

Ripping irresponsible behavior

Writing at his Bearing Arms.com blog, author Bob Owens discussed with disdain an episode involving a Georgia man who strolled into the Atlanta airport carrying an AR-15 rifle, slung across his chest and fitted with a drum magazine. The obviously scornful Owens observed, "…your average citizen isn't going to be able to grasp why a mentally healthy person might want or need to walk into an airport with AR-15 with a drum magazine inserted to see someone off at the airport, unless that airport is in Afghanistan."

He further stated that the man's "fifteen-minute stunt did nothing to help the gun rights movement, and gave gun control supporters ammunition that they will reuse again and again for years to come to portray gun owners as extreme, paranoid, and out of touch with the American mainstream. That's not helping us and never will."

The fallout from this incident was almost immediate. Anti-gun veteran Georgia Congressman Hank Johnson introduced legislation dubbed the "Airport Security Act of 2015." If adopted, it would bar anyone bringing firearms into areas of airports outside the security checkpoints, including those who have a concealed carry license.

Similarly, when a small group of open carriers showed up at a gun rights rally on the capitol steps in Olympia, Washington in January 2015, to join in the protest against the passage the previous November of a "universal background check" initiative. This group broke off from the main crowd and strolled inside of the capitol building, and then up into the viewers' gallery in the House chamber, which was unoccupied at the time, where they posed with raised rifles for a photographer. That image became something of a "poster child" for the Evergreen State gun control crowd, and it also showed up in anti-gun postings in Oregon.

Within days, both the state Senate and House banned the open carry of firearms in either chamber. Open carry had been allowed without challenge for several years. The incident was called "irresponsible" by several in attendance, yet the participants insisted that the flap was all the fault of legislative leaders.

One open carry advocate privately confided that some people have practiced open carry in "a politically toxic manner."

Another veteran open carry advocate in the Pacific Northwest posted a message via social media that seems to state succinctly what many in the movement believe.

Open carry proponent Nick Smith observed, "Every day I get up and drive in Seattle-Tacoma traffic and there are times it scares me and other drivers. However, it is not the vehicle that scares me or others it is the behavior of the driver of that vehicle. I think you will find that it is the behavior of an individual that chooses to open carry that scares others not the firearm…

"For the last couple of years I have carried openly and I will say that 95% of the people in public do not see my firearm," he added. "Why? Because I am polite, courteous, and professional. Furthermore, my behavior invokes trust, not fear in others. I go about my business as though I was concealed. I carry openly for that small percent that do ask and are genuinely curious about the practice and then I am willing to educate and be a positive face to gun owners."

Smith wrote that he has taken the educational approach, trying to demonstrate to others that open carry is not abnormal, while endeavoring to "correct the behavior of others who open carry whose behavior is not polite, courteous, professional and kind."

While openly carrying firearms may never be entirely in vogue again, the reality is that the majority of people who do it are like Smith. They're not attention-seekers, nor do they feel the need for demagoguery.

People like Smith will forever find themselves up against others like the Marine Corps veteran named Troy H. Conrey, who wrote an opinion piece for the *San Antonio Express-News* headlined "Open carry will make us less safe." His opinion: "When it comes to protecting ourselves as a society and protecting our families in public spaces, guns are simply not the right tool for the job. I'm not, in any way, making the argument that citizens should not be able to own guns, but rather that there must be alignment with rights, responsibility and the legislation surrounding where and how a gun can be legally carried."

Perhaps Conrey and Smith, or others like them, will one day have a chance to sit down and discuss their differences.

Whether the practice continues to slowly expand remains to be seen. As the saying goes, "Keep Calm and Carry."

5: CONSTITUTIONAL CARRY

"Carrying a gun is a lifestyle. The government should trust its citizens."—Kansas State Rep. Travis Couture-Lovelady

Considering that the earth didn't change its axis and that the sun still rises in the east, the decision by Kansas Gov. Sam Brownback in 2015 to sign into law what is now generically called a "constitutional carry" measure that allows the carrying of concealed handguns without a permit by anyone age 21 or older must not have been the end of civilization as we know it, after all.

Likewise, Maine did not suddenly fall into depravity when Gov. Paul LePage signed similar legislation in 2015. That law took effect in mid-October, and the state has hardly become a lawless frontier.

When the Constitution was written more than 225 years ago, there was no such thing as a concealed carry permit or license, people often carried rifles, muskets, fowling pieces (shotguns) and even one or two pistols if the occasion called for it. While civilization was beginning to thrive, there was still a frontier, and highwaymen and other ne'er do wells were also a threat.

As civilization advanced and the nation recovered from the Civil War, governments began regulating the carrying of firearms. In some cases, this was aimed at keeping rival political or even criminal factions disarmed, and in other cases in the Deep South, it was designed to keep freed blacks defenseless.

The idea that someone would be required to apply for and get a permit to own, much less carry, a firearm took hold. As such laws spread, many law-abiding citizens simply stopped carrying firearms on a daily basis and the tradition of being armed fell out of vogue.

Through this process, generations of citizens became accustomed to permit systems that were arbitrary and frequently prohibitive in that the law was on the books but permits were rarely given out except to well-connected and wealthy people. Average citizens began going without.

Over the final 20 years of the 20th Century, something happened. Spearheaded by organizations including the National Rifle Association, Citizens Committee for the Right to Keep and Bear Arms, Gun Owners of America, and the Second Amendment Foundation, the wheels were set in motion to regain lost Second Amendment ground.

"Shall-issue" and state preemption laws were adopted to take local politics out of the carry permit process. Lawsuits were filed to challenge various gun laws, and scholarly research was conducted that brought forth a revived interest in the right to keep and bear arms, while keeping the government out of it as much as possible.

Concealed carry expanded to all 50 states, at least in name, and in many of those states, increasing numbers of people went through the process to be legally armed. The open carry movement likewise gained a foothold, and hard-working Second Amendment activists pushed back to regain ground that had been lost gradually over the course of decades.

As a result, a remarkable thing happened. Many activists wondered why anyone should need a permit (government permission slip) to exercise a constitutionally-protected, fundamental civil right. Thus, the "constitutional carry" movement was born.

For decades, the only state in which one could carry a firearm openly or concealed without a permit was Vermont. Gun rights activists clamored for "Vermont style" carry, established by a court ruling that essentially said that no permit or license was required of anyone carrying a firearm openly or concealed in a peaceable manner.

When Kansas adopted its new carry law, State Rep. Travis Couture-Lovelady was quoted by the Associated Press noting, "Kansans already have two documents granting them the right to concealed carry — the Constitution of the United States and the Kansas Constitution. That should be all they need."

Seven of the 50 states at this writing have "Constitutional carry." They are the aforementioned Vermont, Maine and Kansas, plus Alaska, Arizona, Arkansas and Wyoming (for residents), and West Virginia, where it took a veto override in March 2016 to make it happen. One can still get permits to take advantage of laws in other states that recognize permits and licenses from these states, except from Vermont, but in these jurisdictions, it is legal to carry openly or concealed without a card or piece of paper in the wallet.

Legislation has been introduced in other states, but not yet adopted. About the same time Kansas adopted constitutional carry in 2015, West Virginia Gov. Earl Ray Tomblin vetoed a similar measure in that state, drawing the wrath of many gun rights activists, who promised to come back to the issue during the 2016 legislative session.

They did exactly that, with both the House and Senate decisively overriding Tomblin's veto in an embarrassing defeat for the Democrat governor.

Adopting constitutional carry is no small undertaking, and it has many ramifications, some financial and others about government authority.

Abolishing a permit/license requirement could cost state and local governments considerable sums of money because the fees they divided will no longer be available. On the other hand, state and local governments would no longer have to staff offices or licensing divisions to take care of all the paperwork that is involved in a statewide licensing scheme, and those positions can be eliminated from an operating budget. Smaller, less expensive government appeals to a lot of people who may not be devoted one way or the other on the firearms issue, but are interested in reducing their tax burden.

Local police chiefs, and sometimes county sheriffs (though the latter are elected officials and do not care to take unpopular positions against their constituents) lament that a crime fighting tool is lost because they have been able to detain and disarm people in the past who were carrying guns without permits/licenses.

It also removes any training requirement for a license that may have been in place, which is another revenue generator for private business and for the state in the form of B&O and income taxes.

One thing that may hinder adoption of constitutional carry laws is the activist movement, itself, some critics assert. That was the suggestion posited by Bob Owens, blogger at Bearing Arms.com, when he wrote about the legislation in Kansas and West Virginia in early 2015.

"You'll note," Owens observed at the time, "that both Kansas and West Virginia were able to get as far as they have without obnoxious and intentionally provocative open carry demonstrations near schools, in the legislature, or in private businesses that unnecessarily added additional hurdles and gave gun control groups ammunition to fight against us.

"Tactics matter," he added.

"Firearm rights campaigners in other states need to study carefully how the organizations in Kansas and West Virginia are building coalitions," Owens stated. "In both of these states, supporters worked diligently and with resolve, while making sure not to do anything to generate or intensify opposition."

Owens threw in this bit of caution: "Anyone who looks at trends is well aware of the fact that firearms freedom is spreading in all but the most restrictive and liberty-challenged states. The momentum is on our side and legislators in both major parties know it. We will prevail… as long as some of the more "politically challenged" on our side don't get in our way."

The Kansas experience

The Kansas effort began with the introduction of Senate Bill 45, sponsored by State Sen. Jake LaTurner, but it picked up 25 co-sponsors, a majority of the state's 40 senators. There was opposition, as noted in coverage of the story by the *Topeka Capitol Journal*. But in the end, common sense and cooler heads prevailed.

Opponents brought up how many people had seen their concealed carry licenses suspended during the previous year, along with the rather small number of people whose applications were rejected. Still, the numbers did not balance out when compared to the overall number of successful applications and the number of licensed people who had done nothing wrong and carried guns responsibly.

Kansas State Sen. Forrest Knox, an Altoona Republican, was quoted by the *Capitol Journal* noting, "I believe in the Constitution. In America, government should trust its citizens. The Second Amendment is there because citizens shouldn't trust the government."

When Gov. Brownback finally signed the legislation, the press reported it almost like a lament lasting several days leading up to the signing. ABC News quoted two leading Democrats, House Minority Leader Tom Burroughs and Rep. John Wilson, who provided the almost obligatory apprehension about the downside of constitutional carry, while describing both as "gun-rights supporters."

Burroughs, from Kansas City, asserted that his colleagues were "getting caught up in extremism."

Wilson, from Lawrence – the town made famous during the Civil War by being sacked and ravaged by William Clark Quantrill's guerillas in 1863 – observed, "I have concerns with the type of culture that we're creating, when guns are in more places, particularly among children."

One can use this opportunity as an aside to note that the safety of children is often used by anti-gunners as an excuse to oppose some gun rights measure. Children have long been political pawns, and so it is with the Second Amendment debate.

Back on topic, if one cannot find a state legislator to speak against a gun rights law, someone from the

Brady Campaign to Prevent Gun Violence is only a telephone call away. In *Washington Post* discussion about constitutional carry proposals in other states, Brian Malte, the national policy director for the Brady Campaign to Prevent Gun Violence, told a reporter there that "Even if a majority of the legislature or the governor might be in favor of concealed-carry laws, it's generally agreed that having some sort of training or background check is really important."

But this is tantamount to saying no such checks or training now exist and that is demonstrably not true. But anti-gunners looking to gin up public furor for new laws, they often couch arguments in language that makes it appear as there are no such laws currently on the books.

One of the more vocal critics of carry laws is the *Huffington Post's* Mike Weisser, known as "Mike the Gun Guy." He was all over the Kansas constitutional carry statute, creating the impression that training requirements for concealed carry licenses in some states are woefully inadequate. He was miffed that such a law enables "every Tom, Dick, Harry and Francine the ability to carry such lethality around without the slightest proof that they have the mental and physical capacity to keep that lethality under control," to which he added that "isn't to my mind, constitutional carry. It's crazy carry."

Perhaps the *Washington Post* revealed one of the primary reasons that some people energetically oppose constitutional carry. There are no background checks involved because it is a permitless process.

"A Quinnipiac poll...also showed that an overwhelming majority of voters, both Democrat and Republican, support background checks for all gun purchases," the newspaper explained. "A similar majority would also bar people suffering from mental illness from purchasing guns."

How Vermont did it

According to Wikipedia, "the term constitutional carry is a *neologism* for the legal carrying of handgun, either openly or concealed, without the requirement of a government permit. The phrase does not typically refer to the unrestricted carrying of a long gun, a knife, or other weapons. The scope and applicability of such laws or proposed legislation can vary from state to state."

The title essentially refers to the situation in Vermont, where for many years it was the only state in the country that did not require a permit to own or carry a firearm, openly or concealed. This has come to be known as "Vermont-style carry," but as mentioned earlier, it now is the law in a handful of states.

As noted in another Wikipedia entry, the Vermont constitution of 1777 is the oldest of the bunch, and in a 1903 court case known as State v. Rosenthal, the Vermont Supreme Court ruled that an ordinance adopted in the town of Rutland that required a "special permission" in writing from the mayor or police chief to carry a pistol "is inconsistent with and repugnant to the Constitution and the laws of the state, and it is therefore to that extent, void."

Thus it has been in Vermont ever since. And that's how so many Second Amendment activists believe the entire country should be.

However, according to a blogger named Scott Landreth, writing at the Tenth Amendment Center, the notion that the Second Amendment is "your gun permit" is all wet. He observed, "Most of the people who utter these words are well-intended. They are very passionate about their right to keep and bear arms, but I can't help but wonder if they truly understand where rights come from or what the 2nd amendment means."

Even in the firearms fraternity, there is disagreement on whether the right to keep and bear arms may be regulated, and to what extent. That may pose the biggest dilemma within the gun community, and the greatest stumbling block in the effort to actually make Vermont-style carry a reality nationwide. One can understand why there is some disagreement on the right to carry, and on whether this right may be regulated by the states.

"The purpose of the Bill of Rights was to further define and clarify the limits of federal authority," Landreth wrote. "The 2nd amendment (sic) doesn't give anyone the right to keep and bear arms, it simply prohibits the federal government from interfering with that preexisting natural right.

"Furthermore," he continued, "the men who drafted, and more importantly ratified, the US Constitution and the subsequent Bill of Rights intended the 2nd amendment to apply to the FEDERAL government only. NOT to the state governments."

In an 'ideal world'

In an ideal gun rights activist's world, every state would be like Vermont, no questions asked. Local police and sheriff's deputies would instantly know the good guys from the bad guys. That world may be somewhere down the road from Fantasy Land, but it's nowhere on a road map of the United States.

One of the drawbacks of constitutional carry, at least in the eyes of people like the aforementioned Mike "The Gun Guy" Weisser, is that it's not possible to tell the difference between good guys and bad guys all the time. Another problem with getting this type of legislation adopted is one that many in the Second Amendment community seem unable to grasp: Not everyone thinks the way you do. As noted earlier with Landreth's remarks about the Second Amendment being the only necessary permit to carry, that's the kind of reasoning most prone to frustrating disappointment, because legislatures don't simply fall in line with what Second Amendment purists – who don't always agree with one another, incidentally – see as simple logic with a simple solution.

Well-intentioned citizens demonstrating for such a cause, as they did in Rexburg a community in the far southeast region of Idaho, have marched on city hall, literally, or showed up at state legislatures, committee hearings or community meetings. That's democracy in action, but it doesn't always produce the results that gun owners seek. While that may leave many convinced that the system is flawed, or even rigged, against their rights, it's still an affirmation that the people have a right to free speech and representative government, even if the government doesn't always decide issues in your favor.

The concept of constitutional carry is rather new to a lot of people who have, as this and previous chapters have detailed, gotten used to the idea of shall-issue carry licenses or permits in fairly recent times. It will take a while longer to restore a full system under which no permit or license is required, if that can ever happen at all, and possibly some very strategic legal action.

The *Rexburg Standard Journal* covered the demonstration in that community and found sympathy for the concept in State Rep. Ronald Nate, who attended the rally. That's another tactic in the effort to restore carrying firearms without government permission slips. Get politicians on your side.

While there are invariably differing points of view on gun rights, as explained a moment ago, pushing for those rights cannot be done in a vacuum. Activists can get much farther in their efforts by having people on their side who are in government, particularly elected officials.

"It's something that my constituents are letting me know about, and it's something I feel obligated to support and run with, not only because my constituents are asking, but it also happens to be right," Nate told the newspaper.

He even spoke at the rally.

In neighboring Washington state, when Second Amendment activists hold rallies at the capitol in Olympia during the legislative session, politicians turn out to appear and speak as well. These people become the voice of firearms owners in their respective states.

Playing Devil's Advocate

Let's play Devil's Advocate for a moment. Why should people be able to walk around in public carrying a firearm openly or concealed without a license or permit? Securing those documents requires a background check at the very minimum. In many states, a training course is required.

Wouldn't that assure the public that anybody carrying a gun in public at least has some safety training and has been checked out to make certain they aren't crazy or have some kind of criminal background?

How do we prevent the wrong people from carrying guns in public where they could harm or kill innocent citizens?

Why shouldn't police and/or sheriff's deputies be able to approach anyone they see openly carrying a firearm and ask for some identification? Why should anyone openly carrying a firearm refuse to provide such identification?

These are questions that Constitutional Carry advocates may have to address in their endeavor to make this the law of the land. Such questions can be like political quicksand for people who have nothing but platitudes in their tool boxes, and it is insufficient to simply say "The Second Amendment is my carry permit" and blow off the questions.

A *right* to bear arms is just that, a civil right, delineated by the federal and most state constitutions in one form or another. It is *not* a *privilege*. Still, a right must be defended with more than a simplistic insistence that rights need no defense. And the Second Amendment does not affirm any right to be boorish.

Even the Supreme Court noted in its majority opinion in *District of Columbia v. Dick Anthony Heller* that some regulation of firearms is constitutional. Writing for the court, the late Justice Antonin Scalia observed, "Like most rights, the Second Amendment right is not unlimited. It is not a right to keep and carry any weapon whatsoever in any manner whatsoever and for whatever purpose: For example, concealed weapons prohibitions have been upheld under the Amendment or state analogues. The Court's opinion should not be taken to cast doubt on longstanding prohibitions on the possession of firearms by felons and the mentally ill, or laws forbidding the carrying of firearms in sensitive places such as schools and government buildings, or laws imposing conditions and qualifications on the commercial sale of arms."

Constitutional Carry advocates have successfully moved laws in Alaska, Arizona and the other states mentioned earlier in this chapter by working with legislators and being willing to listen to the concerns of opponents. One learns by listening to the opposition, and activists in other states can also learn from the efforts in those states where such legislation has passed.

Restoring the right to carry without a license or permit may take political baby steps. Remember, if at first you don't succeed, try, try again. That's how gun control advocates have pushed through increasingly onerous gun laws, exploiting various tragedies in the process. Reversing years of incremental impairment of the right to carry could take as many years, and involve both court and legislative actions.

A 'national standard?'

Writing at a website called Concealed Nation, blogger James England explained why, in his opinion, concealed carry permits "trump constitutional carry (for now)."

He asserted that permitless concealed carry "hasn't caught on – yet." That's not to suggest that it will not expand, but only a handful of states have adopted it and efforts to push it in other states have failed.

Another reason is that national reciprocity also "hasn't caught on – yet." Focusing on people who travel, he noted, "for those being issued a concealed carry permit, at least they have verified proof at least one state found them fit to carry a concealed firearm. And it also familiarizes the person with his own state's process – which can sometimes be helpful when applying for non-resident concealed carry permits from other states."

"In the grand majority of states, carrying a concealed firearm without a permit is a crime," he says, later adding, "Thus, for those traveling around, it's always a good idea to maintain a concealed carry permit – even if your state doesn't require it. Until we have national reciprocity (which may unfortunately come with national standards), we can't expect any reasonable degree of leniency from non-resident states."

That's an awful big presumption he makes about a national standard being adopted with any kind of national reciprocity bill. There has been no indication that any such standard is in the works, or even that it could pass, because such a standard would never find consensus. Eastern lawmakers would want it to be very restrictive, and western lawmakers outside California would balk.

The more practical approach is to simply require full faith and credit recognition of each state's permit/license by other states.

Ultimately, of course, if constitutional carry could become reality nationwide, this permit process and recognition mandate would disappear. That would be the ideal situation for constitutional carry proponents.

Can you imagine being able to carry a defensive firearm – openly or concealed – while walking through New York City's Times Square?

For that to become a reality will require a considerable amount of work, perhaps a good court case or two, and what Bob Owens earlier in this chapter observed about the importance of sound political tactics. You know, "without obnoxious and intentionally provocative" behavior.

6: GUN-FREE ZONES

"The phrase 'gun-free zone' is liberal for 'sitting duck.' Gun-free is music to the ears of fiends who target the unarmed on purpose"—Greg Gutfeld, host of 'The Five' on Fox News

Nothing so defies logic as the designation of some area, be it a government building, city park or private business establishment as a "gun-free zone."

The fatal shooting in Chattanooga, Tennessee of four U.S. Marines and a U.S. Navy petty officer at a recruiting facility created an explosive controversy when various reports revealed that this facility was a "gun-free" area and that the Marines were unarmed. In at least six states, governors quickly announced that they would authorize full-time military personnel at National Guard facilities to be armed.

That foolishness was underscored four months later by the depravity in San Bernardino at the Inland Regional Center. Fourteen dead and 20 wounded in just a few minutes, in a location where there were not supposed to be any firearms.

And then came the massacre in Orlando. When a homegrown, radicalized terrorist stormed into the Pulse nightclub, he was able to shoot more than a hundred people, and 49 of them perished. Nobody in there had a gun because nobody but the off-duty police officer working security outside the building was allowed to have a gun.

Of course, in the wake of the attack, instead of blaming the terrorist gunman, gun prohibitionists moved quick to capitalize on the incident to blame the Second Amendment.

While the Chattanooga attack, on military personnel, laid bare the utter foolishness of such zones it did not suddenly eliminate them, and that attack will be discussed at greater length later in this chapter. Suffice to say, what happened in Chattanooga caused public attention to focus where it belonged: The absurdity of gun-free zones, and no small credit is due to the photographers who captured images of the shot-up glass door at the recruiting facility, with the "No Guns" allowed sign right in the middle.

Among veteran self-defense experts and advocates, these locations are routinely dismissed with a variety of derisive terms including "risk-free killing zones," "felony enhancement zones," or "zones of happy thoughts." Among those who have studied mass shootings – which have occurred all-too-frequently in places designated as "gun-free" – the notion that one can prevent any violent crime from occurring in such an area is, at best, delusional. Honestly believing that a sign might stop a determined terrorist or psychopath from committing mass mayhem is best described by a term once used by U.S. Rep. Trey Gowdy (R-SC): "mind-numbingly stupid."

Name the sites of the most horrible mass shootings in America: Sandy Hook, Columbine, Fort Hood, the Washington, D.C. Navy Yard, Virginia Tech and on down the line, including the Aurora, Colorado theater that was the scene of the infamous "Batman Massacre," and what they have in common is that each one was a "gun-free zone." Perhaps the one significant exception was the shopping mall in Tucson, Arizona where former Congresswoman Gabrielle "Gabby" Giffords survived an attempted assassination while six other people, including a youngster, were murdered by a gunman who had passed a background check.

Passing background checks seems to be another common denominator in mass shootings. These crazed killers either passed a check, or they stole guns from someone who had. Even Kip Kinkel, the twisted youngster who opened fire at Thurston High School in Springfield, Oregon on May 21, 1998 used guns obtained legally by his father. In the case of the San Bernardino terror couple, their guns were allegedly obtained by a friend in what is traditionally called a "straw purchase." The Orlando gunman had been under FBI surveillance at one time, but the case apparently ended and his name did not pop up as a disqualified person when he bought the gun used in his attack. His record was clean and he passed the background check.

When Fox News host Greg Gutfeld, speaking about shootings at Ft. Hood, Texas during a segment on "The Five," observed, "the phrase 'gun-free zone' is liberal for 'sitting duck.' Gun-free is music to the ears of fiends who target the unarmed on purpose," according to a partial transcript published by Breitbart. com.

He further noted that the scene of the first Ft. Hood shooting by Nidal Hassan "was gun-free at the time of the attack."

According to Breitbart, Gutfelt summed it all up thusly: "Hell, even Media Matters wouldn't put a gun-free sticker on their office window. And for every TV hack dismissing these notions, that's done from a secured perch. They should thank the Second Amendment for protecting the First. Their complacency is a byproduct of a well-armed society, they civility that makes you think massacres can't happen here depends on the armed American who makes those threats costly. Gun-free zones remove that. So, as we witness a new emerging savagery, why not cherish our well-armed independence, why not have our enemies think they're not the only crazies who cling to religion and guns. If you can't beat them, shoot them."

The debate over gun-free zones has been one marked by sneering dismissal toward the notion that armed private citizens might make a difference in any shooting, while on the other hand, anecdotal evidence that an armed response can be and has been effective in such cases is routinely ignored by the mainstream press, which often operates more as a mouthpiece for the gun prohibition lobby than as an objective news medium.

When Mother Jones did an investigation of mass shootings in 2012, the article quoted Dr. Stephen Hargarten, identified as a leading expert on emergency medicine and gun violence at the Medical College of Wisconsin. According to him, the article explained, "There is no evidence indicating that arming Americans further will help prevent mass shootings or reduce the carnage."

The article continued, "Armed civilians attempting to intervene are actually more likely to increase the bloodshed, says Hargarten, 'given that civilian shooters are less likely to hit their targets than police in these circumstances.'"

Many in the firearms community, especially those who have become proficient with their defensive sidearms, might be tempted to suggest that the Mother Jones article is nonsense. While the piece did mention the wild shootout involving New York police officers and a murder suspect in the street near the Empire State Building during which nine bystanders were wounded, it was as if to suggest that, "See, if trained cops can't hit what they're shooting at, neither can armed private citizens."

The article also asserted that of 62 mass shootings identified and analyzed over the past 30 years, "one striking pattern in the data is this: In not a single case was the killing stopped by a civilian using a gun."

But what about mass shootings that were prevented? In December 2007, a Colorado woman named Jeanne Assam, who was a former law enforcement officer and was providing security at the New Life Church in Colorado Springs, shot a man who had just gunned down two teenage sisters outside the building, as he entered to probably continue his rampage inside the sanctuary. That gunman subsequently killed himself, but he was not able to kill any more victims.

According to a fact check by Snopes, accounts of this incident stopping a mass shooting are "mostly true."

In response to the *Mother Jones* article, a writer at *The Weekly Standard* offered a rebuttal, asserting that there were "a couple of major problems" with the argument that armed private citizens don't stop mass shooting. The article then pointed out five such cases, including the Mayan Palace Theater in San Antonio in which a gunman was killed by an off-duty, armed policeman; a restaurant shooting in Winnemucca, Nevada in which the gunman was killed by a private citizen, the famous Appalachian School of Law shooting in 2002 that was interrupted by two armed students, an incident at a high school in Santee, California in which an off-duty police officer who was dropping off his daughter and took the shooter into custody, and Pearl High School in Mississippi, where the vice principal grabbed a handgun from his truck and held the shooter until police arrived. There was also a shooting in Pennsylvania in which a restaurant owner nearby responded with a shotgun when shots were fired at a junior high school dance. The restaurateur killed the gunman.

The *Weekly Standard* article referred to an earlier piece that appeared in *Forbes*, headlined "Disarming the myths promoted by the gun control lobby," in which it was noted that "*Newsweek* has reported that law-abiding American citizens using guns in self-defense during 2003 shot and killed two and one-half times as many criminals as police did, and with fewer than one-fifth as many incidents as police where an innocent person mistakenly identified as a criminal (2% versus 11%)."

Historically, *Newsweek* has never been a staunch pro-Second Amendment publication. The Forbes piece bluntly observed, "As much as gun control advocates might wish otherwise, their attacks are running out of ammo. With private firearm ownership at an all-time high and violent crime rates plunging, none of the scary scenarios they advanced have materialized. Abuse of responsibility by armed citizens is rare, while successful defensive interventions against assaults on their lives and property are relatively commonplace."

Hitting the mall

While approximately 13 million private citizens were licensed to carry when this book was written – and the number was continuing to climb – their legally-carried handguns are, at least theoretically, of no value when they are locked in a car outside a restaurant or shopping mall that is posted against the carrying of firearms. Private property owners can do that, but shootings at shopping malls, such as the December 2012 incident at the Clackamas Town Center outside of Portland, Oregon, just days before the Sandy Hook tragedy at the far end of the country, belie the effectiveness of such prohibitions.

There is a controversy surrounding the Clackamas shooting, as an armed citizen has contended that the gunman in that incident saw him aiming his own handgun but not firing. The armed citizen, Nick Meli, contended that once gunman Jacob Tyler Roberts, who had just killed two innocent bystanders with a stolen rifle, stopped shooting, ran down a hall and committed suicide. According to the account on Wikipedia, "Meli claims that Roberts saw him and that this may have contributed to Roberts' decision to commit suicide. Lt. James Rhodes, Clackamas County Sheriff's Office spokesman, stated that there was no information indicating that the shooter's actions were ever influenced by anything Mr. Meli did."

Many in the firearms community believe the police simply dismissed Meli's role because they did not wish to credit his actions as having anything to do with the sudden decision by Roberts to cease fire and take his own life.

The Clackamas Town Center has a firearms prohibition. One hell of a lot of good that did in preventing Roberts from shooting up the place, whether Meli's intervention stopped the carnage or not. Meli was also in violation of the gun prohibition, but in this case, perhaps two wrongs did make a right.

Another incident years earlier at the Tacoma Mall in neighboring Washington state is one that anti-gunners like to use in order to buttress their argument against allowing armed customers in gun-free zones. In 2005 when a young gunman opened fire at the popular mall, an employee at one of the shops drew his own legally-carried handgun, approached the gunman and ordered him to lay down his rifle. Instead, Dominic Maldonado shot Brendan (Dan) McKown, disabling him.

However, McKown's intervention, though it worked out poorly for the good Samaritan, may have been pivotal, because afterwards, the gunman retreated into a store, no more shots were apparently fired and he ultimately surrendered to police. Nobody was killed at the Tacoma Mall, but several people were injured.

The moral to this story is simple, according to many in the firearms community: When there is an active shooter and you are armed, and have a clear shot, don't challenge him verbally. Just shoot him and stop the mayhem. Once a gunman is down, the police can sort out the details.

Gun-free illusion

In the years since the tragic Columbine High School massacre in 1999, some parents have become staunch gun control advocates. But the gun-free zone illusion did not prevent that tragedy. By that time, gun free school zones were already the law. Originally passed in 1990 and championed by then-Sen. Joe Biden, the first one was signed into law by then-President George H.W. Bush.

Gun control activists seem to consistently ignore this historical fact, acting instead as though there was no law against carrying firearms on a school campus.

But at least one person who was at Columbine, and went on to become a state representative in the Colorado Legislature, had a different perspective than the anti-gunners. Patrick Neville was 15 years old on that tragic day and told NPR that, while many teachers acted "heroically," he thinks they should have had the tools to fight back.

"I truly believe that had some of them had the legal authority to be armed, more of my friends might be with me today," he said in an interview.

He put those thoughts into action, sponsoring legislation in Colorado that would make it legal for anyone with a concealed carry license to carry in a public school. There's more to that than simple posturing.

As in other states, people who obtain a carry permit in Colorado go through a background check. There is also a training requirement.

Bolstering Neville's effort was a 2014 poll done by Quinnipiac University that revealed half of Coloradoans favor arming teachers, NPR noted. Forty-five percent oppose the idea, including a third grade teacher identified as Katie Lyles. Her opinion was that, "I feel like we need to be looking at a different conversation. And that conversation is, how do we prevent violence from even entering that school."

That's an idea with some merit, but that doesn't offer a solution to an immediate emergency if an active shooter is already inside the building. By then, the time for preventive measures has passed.

Neville, discussing school students with the NPR reporter, had this observation: "They're just easy targets

... for a criminal, a terrorist or anyone intent on doing harm. I wake up every day and send my kid to school on blind faith that she's going to return home safe when there's really no safeguards for our schools."

NPR noted that similar legislation was proposed in neighboring Wyoming, with Assemblyman Allen Jaggi spearheading the effort. He told NPR what so many other people have said time and again about mass shootings: They have occurred almost entirely in so-called "gun-free" zones. While NPR threw in a caveat that this correlation between mass shootings and gun-free zones is "not entirely true," the fact remains that such places seem to be magnets for violence.

Jaggi told the news agency that making it legal for guns to be carried at school just might have a deterrent effect. There are those who disagree vehemently with this position, but there is no evidence that there has been any kind of violent attack at any school or institution that has adopted a guns-on-campus policy with enough publicity that people would know they might be up against armed resistance.

Cops support carry

Writing in *National Review* in early 2014, veteran firearms data researcher and author Dr. John Lott discussed the "cruelty" of gun-free zones, and he was rather to the point. The president of the Crime Prevention Research Center, Lott noted, "Law enforcement recognizes that gun-free zones leave shooting victims defenseless." He then proceeded to explain how the concept of a gun-free zone played into the hands of both Adam Lanza, the Sandy Hook mass killer, and James Holmes, who was ultimately convicted for opening fire and killing several people at the theater in Aurora.

Lott reported that, "The vast majority of mass shootings in the U.S. have been extensively planned beforehand — often many months or even years in advance, allowing the perpetrators to find unprotected targets and obtain weapons." Lanza, according to Lott, spent two years studying mass shootings and Holmes had spent months buying guns and ammunition, and also visiting neighborhood theaters, buying a ticket to the movie premiere a couple of weeks in advance.

Investigators looking at the San Bernardino terror attack reportedly learned that months had also been apparently spent planning that outrage, and another attack that was not carried out.

Lott also offered this observation: "Holmes appears to have carefully selected the theater he did: Seven theaters within a 20-minute drive of his apartment were showing the premier of The Dark Knight Returns. He chose the only one posting signs banning concealed guns — not the theater closest to his apartment or the one prominently advertising the largest auditoriums in Colorado."

This kind of small detail may not seem significant to some people, but to armed citizens and Lott, it is very important and it underscores the long-standing suspicion that many mass shooters carefully pick their targets to find the spots that offer the smallest odds of resistance, especially *armed* resistance.

If one considers Lott's assessment to be even partly correct – and the places we mentioned earlier in this chapter certainly seem to support his thesis – gun-free zones just might be among the most dangerous places on the landscape.

Lott had some key validation for his position from PoliceOne, an organization with some 450,000 active duty and retired law enforcement members. In a survey conducted in March 2013, just a few months after Sandy Hook and the Clackamas mall shooting, the group asked this question: "What would help most in preventing large scale shootings in public?"

According to PoliceOne, "The most popular answer among respondents – at 29 percent – was 'more permissive concealed carry policies for civilians,' while 20 percent choose 'more-aggressive institutionalization for mentally ill persons'."

You did not read about this survey, or its results anywhere in the mainstream press. The revelations did not follow the gun control narrative to which the media seem to subscribe. Perhaps one reason is because this was so soon after the Newtown outrage, and the survey revealed that "a full 86 percent feel that casualties would have been reduced or avoided in recent tragedies like Newtown and Aurora if a legally-armed citizen was present (casualties reduced: 80 percent; avoided altogether: 60 percent)."

The law enforcement professionals who answered this survey, some 15,000 of them, also contended that another strategy for addressing mass shootings was "More aggressive institutionalization for mentally ill persons."

How does the gun prohibition lobby deal with something like this, especially when it claims to have law enforcement on its side?

Easy, they simply ignore it, probably realizing that the sympathetic mainstream press will do likewise. As noted earlier, that's essentially what happened...or *didn't* happen, depending upon one's perspective.

The author of the PoliceOne article was former cop Ron Avery, president and director of training for the practical Shooting Academy, Inc., and executive director of the non-profit Rocky Mountain Tactical Institute. In his article, Avery noted that more than 81 percent of the survey respondents supported the notion of having armed teachers and/or school administrators, provided they were "properly trained and vetted or at least proficient."

Perhaps not surprisingly, Avery acknowledged that most teachers and administrators were not keen on the idea.

"Overcoming this kind of resistance will be a major roadblock to making our schools safer," Avery wrote at the time.

True enough. A large segment of school teachers and administrators are anti-gun, or at least of the liberal political persuasion which traditionally supports gun control measures. But for a group that pushes education, this group seems rather resistant to the kind of learning opportunity that might save their lives and the lives of their students.

Writing also about gun-free zones for Fox News in the spring of 2015, Dr. Lott looked at two surveys that came up with remarkably different results on the subject of firearms and self-defense. One survey was conducted by Professor David Hemenway at Harvard, a fellow whose name occasionally appears in connection with gun control issues.

The other survey was done by Professor Gary Mauser at Simon Fraser University. His name occasionally is associated with pro-rights research.

According to Lott, the Hemenway effort "polled authors who had published in the fields of 'public health, public policy, sociology, or criminology.' Most notably, half of the authors picked were within Hemenway's own field of public health and another third were sociologists/criminologists, followed by public policy and a few economists. It dramatically over weighted those in public health. It didn't matter whether the publications even contained any empirical work or were related to the survey questions."

On the other hand, Mauser polled "economics researchers."

So, how did the two efforts turn out? Hemenway's survey found that 73 percent of the respondents disagreed with the statement, "In the United States, guns are used in self-defense far more often than they are used in crime."

However, Mauser's survey came up with this result: "88 percent of North American economics researchers agreed with the statement that, in the US, guns were more frequently used for self-defense than for crime."

How is it possible that the survey results were so different? As Lott put it, "It is abundantly clear that it matters who you ask and how the questions are asked."

Lott's article was in response to a report in the Boston Globe a week earlier about Hemenway's research. That piece noted that, "A majority of gun researchers believe that strong gun laws help reduce homicide and that a gun in someone's home can make it a more dangerous place, according to recent surveys conducted by Harvard University."

The Boston Globe portrayed Hemenway's respondents as "experts," and noted that "A majority also said they believe having a gun in the home increases the risk of suicide and the risk that a woman living in the home will become a victim of homicide."

Carrying on campus

In April 2015, The Outdoor Channel aired its first-ever documentary, and it was a direct smack at the gun-free zone concept. Keep in mind this special aired before the shootings at Chattanooga, Colorado Springs and San Bernardino. Suffice to say, We Were Warned. Titled "Safe Haven: Gun-Free Zones in America," the program asked whether such areas are really safe. The answer is a resounding "No" and all the proof one needs are the body counts from each crime scene.

One of the people appearing in the episode was Amanda Collins, a concealed carry permit holder and survivor of sexual assault, who simply asks, "How does rendering me defenseless protect you against a violent crime?"

Collins was the woman who, when testifying in Colorado against gun control legislation there in 2013, found herself being lectured by then-state Sen. Evie Hudak, an anti-gun Democrat, that statistics were against her if she had tried to defend herself with a gun. Quickly criticized for her insensitive remarks, Hudak subsequently apologized, but the damage had been done. Months later, she resigned her senate seat rather than be recalled.

Collins, on the other hand, told her story again, noting pointedly that, "Eventually the man who raped me, James Biela, was caught. He was tried and convicted for not only raping me at gun point in a gun-free zone, but also raping two other women and murdering Brianna Denison." She noted in an Op-Ed response to a column written for MSNBC by celebrity anti-gunner Shannon Watts, head of Mom's Demand Action for Gun Sense in America, that, "The laws need to change so that those who have a valid concealed carry permit can lawfully bring their firearms onto college campuses, just as they do elsewhere in their daily lives. I know from my personal experience that threats to personal safety don't magically disappear in declared 'safe-zones.'"

It is rather difficult to argue with someone having Collins' experience, as Hudak learned the hard way.

Another person featured was J. Eric Deitz, identified as a homeland security researcher at Purdue University's College of Technology. His observation about gun-free zones should open some eyes: "It appears that (criminals) are seeking a spot that will keep them from being prevented in accomplishing their mission…If their mission is mass casualties, they're going to want to be undisturbed in that process until they've completed it."

None of this seems to matter to stubborn opponents of campus carry, as illustrated by a former professor at the University of Arkansas, who authored a guest commentary on the subject for the Arkansas Online version of the *Arkansas Democrat-Gazette*. Retired Prof. Samuel Totten criticized a campus carry proposal in Arkansas as "not only alarming but muddleheaded."

In his short essay, Totten trotted out all the bogeyman arguments against firearms on campus, from carelessness by student gun-toters to the potential of loss or theft. He includes a lament about possible harm to bystanders from stray bullets in the event of a gun battle.

"(I)t is not unheard of," he wrote, "for faculty members to get into very heated arguments, sometimes to the point of almost engaging in fisticuffs. Likewise, it is not unheard of to have faculty or staff members on college/university campuses who have mental problems and/or are hotheads or lacking in common sense. Evidence? Three examples shall have to suffice: In July 1976, a library custodian at California State University, Fullerton killed eight people on campus. In May 2009, a University of Alabama professor shot and killed three people and wounded three others during a faculty meeting. In September 2014, a professor at Idaho state was wounded when the pistol he had in his pocket accidentally discharged."

While the theft argument has merit, the thought of some wild shootout involving armed staff and/or adult students seems a bit far-fetched.

The first two of Totten's examples possibly could have been interrupted and/or stopped cold by a legally-armed student or another staff member, while the third case involved a mishap that could happen anywhere if someone is careless with his or her firearm.

There was another Op-Ed piece from an academic that appeared in the *Daily Record* in Parsippany, New Jersey, where James Alan Fox, the Lipman Professor of Criminology, Law and Public Policy at Northeastern University, wrote, "Combating campus sexual assault is clearly an important goal for college administrations, and there are some reasonable steps to take, including better control of alcohol consumption. But allowing guns on campus will only create more problems." What problems might be created when someone fights back?

Fox, a member of *USA Today's* Board of Contributors, asserted that much of the discussion about campus rape is "hype and hysteria — far out of proportion with the actual risk…"

That, of course, depends upon one's perspective. Amanda Collins and others like her who are the actual victims of sexual assault on campus would argue that her odds of being attacked had hit 100 percent, and nothing Prof. Fox had to say could alleviate that one bit.

Business establishments that conspicuously post themselves off-limits to firearms with signs on doors or in windows are often shunned by gun rights and self-defense activists for this very reason. They do not care to support businesses where they have reason to fear becoming a defenseless victim.

Some of the big box warehouse stores have no-guns policies, but armed citizens simply ignore the signs and carry, anyway. Many believe that such places should be held liable for any injuries suffered by any patrons who somehow become crime victims when they have been disarmed.

For the self-defense advocate, there can be no sound reason to create a gun-free zone, other than being convinced that the false sense of security is either a) actually genuine, or b) politically correct. Many businesses succumb to political correctness, or to pressure from groups like Watts' Moms Demand Action, which is supported by anti-gun billionaire Michael Bloomberg, or on advice from corporate attorneys about possible liability associated with allowing armed customers into their establishments without some attempt to discourage them.

The greater liability potential would appear to be from law-abiding citizens who must leave their guns in the car or at home, and wind up being crime victims.

Chattanooga outrage

As noted earlier in this chapter, what should have been a proverbial "game changing" moment in the controversy over so-called "gun-free zones" exploded in headlines when a lone gunman opened fire on two military recruiting facilities in the Chattanooga, Tennessee area, killing four U.S. Marines and a U.S. Navy petty officer at one of the locations before becoming embroiled in a gun battle with local police.

Mohammad Youssuf Abdulazeez was deadly against unarmed military personnel, but when he came up against armed Chattanooga cops, his fortunes changed abruptly and forever. He was killed in the shootout.

Likewise, San Bernardino radicalized terrorists Syed Rizwan Farook and his wife, Tashfeen Malik, found easy pickings in the unarmed, target-rich environment of the Inland Regional Center. However, a couple of miles away, and about four hours later, they were stopped cold by a hail of police bullets, saving California and federal taxpayers the expense of prosecution.

The Chattanooga incident in particular did not merely rekindle a debate about the efficacy of "gun-free" signs, it left gun prohibitionists scrambling to deflect public attention away from the discussion altogether. What that incident underscored, thanks primarily to one image that has become iconic, is that good intentions do not stop people with bad intent. It is the image of the bullet-riddled glass front doors of the recruiting office with bullet holes all around a sign showing the typical gun over which a red circle with diagonal bar has been placed that signifies guns are not allowed inside.

As noted by author Workman, "(People) are rapidly understanding that crazy mass shooters or hate-driven terrorists are more effectively stopped with return fire than they are by waiving a 'Gun-Free Zone' sign in their face."

Republican Presidential candidate Donald Trump made hay with the Chattanooga attack and image of the sign in the shot-up door, calling the disarming of American troops in military facilities ridiculous and disgraceful.

But then it was revealed that bans on weapons at recruiting centers have been in effect at least since 1993, and that this prohibition followed a "directive" from President George H.W. Bush the previous year that had actually created the gun-free zones on military bases. Bill Clinton expanded on it, according to the *New York Daily News* account, although these reports were challenged by some people who insist the prohibition dated back to the Civil War. There is a general prohibition on firearms inside federal offices and places where federal employees work.

However this regulation was put in place, the Chattanooga shooting brought it under well-deserved scrutiny.

Chris Cox, executive director of the NRA's Institute for Legislative Action, released a statement that reflected the consensus opinion about this disarmament.

"It's outrageous," Cox observed, "that members of our Armed Services have lost their lives because the government has forced them to be disarmed in the workplace. President Obama should fully repeal Defense Department Directive 5210.56 immediately, and Congress should pursue a legislative fix to ensure that our service men and women are allowed to defend themselves on U.S. soil."

As quickly as they could, anti-gunners exploited the attack to call for more gun control laws, rather than engage in a discussion about "gun-free zones" that they have promoted, and which have proven to be universal failures when it comes to preventing harm to anyone inside.

The story quoted Kelli Bland, public affairs chief for the U.S. Army Recruiting Command Center, who said "we go by policy." But then later in the story, she explained that these centers "are in public spaces. Applicants need to feel comfortable. They're not there to get a rehearsal to join the Army."

It is not possible to feel comfortable if some loon or would-be lone wolf terrorist starts shooting at you through the glass doors.

In the immediate wake of the Chattanooga shooting, some recruiting offices in several different states suddenly found themselves protected, albeit temporarily, by armed private citizen volunteers, including some veterans. That was something of an embarrassing development, not only for gun control proponents, but also for a military high command that kept its personnel disarmed even in the wake of two shootings at Fort Hood, Texas and a third at the U.S. Navy Shipyard in Washington, D.C.

General Ray Odierno, chief of staff of the Army, did not earn any points when he told reporters, "I think we have to be careful about over-arming ourselves, and I'm not talking about where you end up attacking each other." According to a Fox News report, the general said there is a concern about "accidental discharges and everything else that goes along with having weapons that are loaded that causes injuries."

Days after the Chattanooga shooting, the *Navy Times* and *Washington Post* reported that a Navy officer and one of the slain Marines may have been armed and did return fire. However, as the Washington Post noted, "According to the Marine unit's commanding officer, Maj. Mike Abrams, Marines are not authorized to carry personally owned firearms while at the support center." A Glock pistol was reportedly found near one of the slain Marines.

The *Navy Times* story reported that the commander at the support center apparently used a personal sidearm to return fire. The publication noted that "it is against Defense Department policy for anyone other than military police or law enforcement to carry weapons on federal property."

Incidentally, in those three earlier cases, each of the shooters had passed background checks during the retail purchases of their firearms.

Weighing in on the Chattanooga attack, Dr. John Lott (mentioned earlier) noted in a column for Fox News that, "We trust soldiers to carry guns all the time when they are stationed in Iraq or Afghanistan, but somehow when they come home we no longer trust them... The Obama administration hasn't learned anything from the massacres at Fort Hood in 2009 and 2014 or the Washington Navy Yard in 2013."

Lott noted the coincidence of the Chattanooga shooting with the delivery of a guilty verdict in the trial of James Holmes, the mass killer from the Aurora, Colorado movie theater, the case discussed earlier in this chapter. Holmes' insanity defense didn't wash with the general public, nor did it impress the jury.

One positive thing that came out of the controversy is that U.S. Senator Jerry Moran of Kansas introduced legislation that would allow active duty military to carry private sidearms at domestic military installations in reaction to the Chattanooga shooting. In a statement, the Republican senator observed, "The U.S. Constitution guarantees the 'right of the people to keep and bear arms shall not be infringed,' yet our men and women in uniform are being prevented from exercising this constitutional right when fulfilling their duties on American soil."

Criminals don't obey the law

Perhaps the absurdity of gun-free zones can best be illustrated by a story that came out of Seattle in mid-2015 about how police detectives, working with the Puget Sound Regional Crime Gun Taskforce, discovered that the same 9mm-caliber pistol had been used in ten shootings in the Seattle area over the course of two years. The revelation also appeared in the *Seattle Times*, which was reporting a broader story about a spike in shootings in parts of the Queen City.

While the story also revealed one major flaw in the gun control philosophy – that criminals can be deterred by ratcheting down on the rights of law-abiding gun owners – it seemed to surprise everyone (perhaps with the exception of gun owners) that inner city thugs might use the same gun to commit multiple offenses, and they're not impressed with gun-free zones or efforts to curve violent crime.

Recall that the City of Seattle had tried to ban guns by administrative regulation in 2009, for which the city was promptly sued by the Second Amendment Foundation, National Rifle Association, Citizens Committee for the Right to Keep and Bear Arms, Washington Arms Collectors and five individual plaintiffs. The city lost at trial and on appeal, but had the city won, the prohibition still would not have prevented the thugs with that 9mm pistol from shooting up the parks.

That incontrovertible fact seems to escape gun prohibitionists; no matter what law is passed, criminals will ignore it.

When a police department spokesman noted that, "We don't know who these guys are. We do know one of the guns involved in this specific shooting has been linked to nine other shootings. It's imperative we get these guns off the streets," it left people wondering if getting the bad guys off the street was just as "imperative."

Across the country in the "other Washington," people in the nation's capital criticized that city's tight restrictions on concealed carry permits following the slaying of a man on a Metro train over the Fourth of July holiday. Kevin Joseph Sutherland was stabbed about 40 times as horrified onlookers did nothing because they were unarmed.

Lars Dalseide, an NRA spokesman, said at the time, "With so many threats in the nation's capital, the fact that the District of Columbia government continues to deny residents and visitors the right to protect themselves is a travesty. We'll continue to hear stories like this until the District of Columbia affords every law-abiding citizen their constitutional right to self-protection."

Breaking the city's bureaucratic strangle hold on carry permits was the object of two Second Amendment Foundation lawsuits, *Palmer v. District of Columbia* and *Wrenn v. District of Columbia*. The first case forced the city to start issuing permits for carry outside the home, and the second challenged the city's onerous "need" requirement that was designed to discourage people and allow most others to be denied.

Humorously, when SAF won the first round in *Wrenn*, the city began issuing permits to anyone who could prove membership in the foundation. Even Dick Anthony Heller, the main plaintiff in the 2008 Second Amendment case, got a membership in SAF and showed that to the city police, and he was promptly issued a permit.

The Second doesn't apply?

One case involving a Colorado man's challenge of a ban on firearms in or on Post Office property could have far-reaching implications. In *Bonidy et al v. United States Postal Service et al*, a case brought by Tad and Debbie Bonidy, Tad had sued the USPS over a ban on guns in the parking lot.

A resident of rural Colorado, Bonidy had to come to the nearest town to pick up his mail because there was no delivery at his residence. He carried a gun with him on these trips to town, and felt that the Second Amendment protected his right to bear arms. He opposed the ban on firearms on all postal property.

He initially won at trial, but on appeal, the decision was reversed by the U.S. Circuit Court of Appeals for the Tenth Circuit. As the NRA portrayed the ruling, "The Tenth Circuit, however, ruled that the Second Amendment does not apply to 'government buildings' and that this term includes the post office parking lot at issue in the case."

Post offices are "gun-free" zones because some years ago, there was a series of shootings at postal facilities, hence the slang term "going postal." This refers to a postal employee opening fire on managers and co-workers over some grievance, real or perceived.

The Appeals Court panel ruled that under the dicta language of the Supreme Court rulings in *District of Columbia v. Dick Anthony Heller* and *McDonald v. City of Chicago*, firearms can be prohibited in so-called "sensitive areas." The Tenth Circuit held that a post office facility is such a "sensitive area" and that a prohibition is presumptively lawful."

But the court also applied the prohibition to the parking lot, which critics asserted was a tremendous reach. If such a ruling is allowed to stand, then the federal government could prohibit firearms in parking lots in national parks and outside other federal offices, including Forest Service ranger stations, which are often visited by hunters, fishermen and other recreationists carrying firearms for outdoor use, simply because firearms are not allowed inside those facilities.

Fighting with common sense

Shortly after the Chattanooga attack caused everyone's focus to settle on "gun-free zones," the Gun Owners' Action League of Massachusetts (GOAL) worked with state Rep. John C. Velis, a Westfield Democrat, to introduce legislation regarding such zones in the Bay State.

The legislation was aimed at analyzing gun-free zone laws, not necessarily amending or repealing them, but it was at least a start in a state not terribly friendly to the Second Amendment. That's ironic, because the

Revolutionary War started in Massachusetts, with the Boston Tea Party and the battles of Lexington and Concord, and Breeds (Bunker) Hill.

But reflecting the sentiments expressed at the beginning of this chapter, GOAL Executive Director Jim Wallace noted in a press release that, "Over the last decade it has become evident that these so-called gun free zones have actually become 'no defense zones'. Tragically they have also become targets for terrorists and murderers."

He also stated the obvious: "Citizens of all walks of life whether in uniform or not should have the right to defend themselves and others any place they have the right to be. It is our hope that this legislation be passed immediately so work can begin to make the Commonwealth a safer place."

Meanwhile, down in Alabama, DeKalb County Sheriff Jimmy Harris circulated a letter to his constituents that left no doubt where he stood on the right to keep and bear arms for personal protection. Bluntly, Sheriff Harris urged people to "put your faith in God...(and) learn to protect yourself by learning the proper and safe ways to handle a weapon."

The sheriff's letter observed, "When people can walk into schools, movie theaters, recruiting stations, etc., and pull out a gun, it's time for all of us law-abiding citizens to take a look at how we protect ourselves, family and friends." And, he suggested that people improve their skills by getting self-defense training.

By no small coincidence, the newspaper reporting this story was the *Chattanooga Times Free Press*, which did extensive coverage of the Marine recruit center shooting only days before.

The victims in Chattanooga did not die in vain, as it turned out. That shooting caused, and will continue to cause, people to reconsider the logic of establishing any area as a "gun-free zone." The Chattanooga recruiting centers that were shot up by a would-be jihadi terrorist should serve as monuments to the foolishness of the far left, that putting up a sign is going to somehow deter dangerous people from causing mass mayhem.

At the very least, such zones should not apply to anyone who is licensed to carry. Ideally, there would be no "gun-free zones" other than prisons and mental hospitals. That could be a worthwhile goal for Second Amendment activists to pursue.

7: STAND YOUR GROUND

"In no states are you allowed to shoot someone who is simply shouting at you or moving towards you loudly and aggressively, unless you reasonably believe that you're in danger of death, serious bodily injury, or the other harms I listed." – Eugene Volokh, UCLA law professor

Possibly the most misunderstood, and certainly the most misrepresented (by anti-gun activists) facet of self-defense law and the right to keep and bear arms is what we commonly call the right to "stand your ground."

Perhaps the origin of this philosophy dates back to April 19, 1775 when, according to popular history, Captain John Parker told his assembled militia men on the village commons at Lexington to "Stand your ground, don't fire unless fired upon..." Even if that's not exactly what was said, it certainly sounds good.

Under such a law, there is no duty to retreat from an attack that occurs in any place where you have a right to be. The Washington State Supreme Court even noted in an opinion called *State v. Reynaldo Redmond* that, "The law is well settled that there is no duty to retreat when a person is assaulted in a place where he or she has a right to be." While that applies to Evergreen State legal history, it pretty much covers how stand your ground self-defense works everywhere it is in effect.

The case that put stand your ground (SYG) on the proverbial map was the shooting of Trayvon Martin by George Zimmerman. Yet, it was an error on the part of the press to even bring the SYG principle into the discussion because that was never a defense issue, and they either knew it and didn't care, or were too stupid to understand it, and didn't really want to.

The fact was that Zimmerman could not have retreated if he had wanted to, and he wasn't standing his ground, he was laying on it, with Martin on top, beating him furiously and possibly even trying to grab his gun. That's what the evidence showed, and it's what the jury decided.

SYG laws have long been a target of the liberal left because they have allowed armed private citizens to avoid punishment for defending themselves with lethal force against dangerous criminals. One thing about many on the radical extreme left side of politics that is consistent is that they don't like it when some citizen fights back and puts down a thug.

Perhaps it has to do with a subconscious fear of someone willing to stand and fight; someone who is self-reliant and skilled in art of self-defense. The short version: Someone who will not be pushed around. You know, some law-abiding citizen *with a gun*.

There are so many anecdotal cases of people defending themselves with lethal force that it would be impossible to list even a small percentage of such cases in this chapter. But one situation that occurred in April 2015 provides an example that some will say really offers no such proof, and others will explain why there is value in a law that does not require an attempt to retreat before using force.

Many self-defense experts will observe that being required to retreat or run from an attack is a pretty good way to get shot or stabbed in the back.

A store employee in Houston, Texas was coming to work one morning with a bag under his arm. The would-be armed robber apparently figured he had an easy target, but as in most of these cases, he made one of those "fatal errors in the victim-selection process."

The bad guy approached the store employee from behind, according to an account by KTRK, the local ABC affiliate, and demanded the bag. But this employee was licensed to carry, and managed to pull his own gun, quickly firing four rounds at the man, fatally wounding him in the chest.

Was the armed employee standing his ground? In a manner of speaking, of course, though he did not have an option of flight; had he seen the robber coming, and then drawn rather than try to flee inside the building, that would have been a textbook example of SYG at work.

Eugene Volokh writes a blog called *The Volokh Conspiracy*. A former computer programmer, he teaches free speech law, tort law and religious freedom law at the UCLA School of Law. He also does clinics on First Amendment amicus briefs, and he has authored textbooks and law review articles. He once clerked for now-retired Supreme Court Justice Sandra Day O'Connor and Judge Alex Kozinski on the U.S. Court of Appeals for the Ninth Circuit.

Writing for the *Washington Post* in June 2014, Volokh took a very hard look at SYG and reminded people that this legal principle does not allow or encourage vigilante behavior if you carry a firearm for personal protection in public.

"In no states," he cautioned at the time, "are you allowed to shoot someone who is simply shouting at you or moving towards you loudly and aggressively, unless you reasonably believe that you're in danger of death, serious bodily injury, or the other harms I listed."

SYG does not give anyone the right to use force simply in reaction to an insult or boorish behavior. It does allow someone to resort to physical self-defense in the event that one is attacked or conclusively threatened with physical harm or death by someone who has the means and proximity to carry out such a threat.

But even then one must exercise self-restraint. As Volokh put it in his article, "What if you just feel fearful for your life, but it's not reasonable for you to feel such fear (again, of death, serious bodily injury, etc.), and you shoot and kill the person you fear? In some states, that would still be murder; in others, it will still be a crime, but a lesser one, usually called involuntary manslaughter or negligent homicide. But of course if your fear is unreasonable, a jury might conclude that it was insincere, too (even given that the prosecution must disprove your defense beyond a reasonable doubt, in all states but Ohio)."

The fear must be genuine but not unreasonable. How does one prove that? Perhaps that will be one of the great mysteries of life, because what is genuine to some may be unreasonable to others, and it may also depend upon the jurisdiction and local laws of self-defense.

One thing has become abundantly clear over the years. There can be no claim of outright self-defense by a person who is a willful participant in what escalates into a lethal confrontation. That is, you cannot dare somebody to "step outside" and then claim you acted in self-defense.

Volokh narrowly defined some parameters of SYG and self-defense, noting that "if you're in the fortunately very rare scenario in which you reasonably believe that the person outside the clinic will imminently shoot you, you can shoot him in any state (if you've got a gun, that is)."

But Volokh continued, "And if you're in the much more common scenario in which you just think the person might slap you or block your entrance or insult you, you can't shoot him in any state. Only in the very rare scenario in which you think the person might kill or seriously injure you, but with a deadly weapon that you can flee with perfect safety would it matter whether you're in a stand-your-ground state or a duty-to-retreat state."

The Zimmerman lesson

Don't confuse SYG with the "Castle Doctrine," which far too many in the mainstream press did after the Treyvon Martin/George Zimmerman confrontation. The two have some connection, but they are not one and the same, and one is left sometimes to wonder if the confusion isn't deliberate on the media's part.

Castle Doctrine is actually a legal doctrine that provides protections to people inside their place of residence, as detailed by a lengthy discussion in Wikipedia. While not exactly defined in statute in all corners of the nation, Colorado instituted such a law in 1985 that was quickly dubbed the "Make My Day" statute because it protected people who used lethal force against home invaders. Opponents nicknamed the law as something of a sneering reference to line spoken by the "Harry

Callahan" character of Clint Eastwood's "Dirty Harry" series.

The concept that "a man's home is his castle" really doesn't equate with SYG outside the home, which is where a lot of self-defense cases occur. While the Castle Doctrine does provide for "no duty to retreat" when attacked in one's own home, the concept of SYG laws is that they provide for some of the same protections away from the residence.

That is, as explained earlier, one does not have a responsibility to retreat from an attack that happens in any place where the intended victim has a right to be.

Remember, in some cases, there is no opportunity or option to retreat. There is only the choice of fighting back or submitting, possibly to being killed.

Neither SYG or Castle Doctrine allows the wanton killing of someone, despite what may have been intimated by anti-self-defense advocates. Certain standards and parameters of self-defense must be met. Recall what Volokh said in the quote earlier in this chapter. Neither of these principles or statutes translates to a hunting license, and to suggest they do is wrong, if not dishonest.

As to SYG specifically, there are laws in 22 states, according to Wikipedia, and in Washington State, a series of court rulings dating back nearly a century have affirmed that there is no duty to retreat in the Evergreen State. However, once again a self-defense claim would have to be supported by the facts. One simply cannot throw one's self in harm's way and then claim self-defense on an SYG argument.

Researcher and economist Dr. John Lott, mentioned previously in this text, has suggested that murder rates fall in states with SYG and Castle Doctrine laws, while opponents of either concept disagree. It may be much the same as the dispute between rights supporters and anti-gunners when discussing the broader right-to-carry issue. Pro rights advocates have and will continue to argue that concealed carry and SYG laws have contributed to overall reductions in crime, while the gun prohibition lobby insists that murder and violent crime rates actually go up in jurisdictions with solid right-to-carry protections and good self-defense statutes.

Wikipedia noted that an analysis of SYG laws at Georgia State that used numbers from the U.S. Vital Statistics determined that there has been a "significant" rise in homicides and injuries among white males.

District attorneys around the country have also not been keen toward SYG laws, and there is a suspicion that some criminals have used the defense to escape prosecution for homicide.

In early 2014, Mark Hoekstra, an associate professor of economics at Texas A&M wrote a lengthy article for Reuters that openly questioned whether SYG laws contribute to increased numbers of homicides. He opened the article by discussing the trial of a Florida man who shot a teen after an argument over loud music. Hoekstra also touched on the Trayvon Martin-George Zimmerman case and wondered whether either of these cases would have happened without an SYG statute in Florida.

The actual research conducted by Hoekstra and colleague Cheng Cheng was published in the *Journal of Human Resources*, and headlined "Does Strengthening Self-Defense Law Deter Crime or Escalate Violence? Evidence from Expansions to Castle Doctrine."

Hoekstra and Cheng noted that from 2000 to 2010, more than 20 states adopted SYG or Castle Doctrine statutes. Their 44-page report suggested that the laws do not deter crimes such as aggravated assault, robbery or burglary, and that they may actually contribute to a net increase in the number of reported murders and non-negligent manslaughters.

It must be justifiable

One question that few people ever try to address in the debates about such laws is whether the decedent "had it coming." That is, if someone is fatally shot, stabbed, bludgeoned or beaten to death, or is fatally injured in a physical confrontation, was his conduct leading up to the confrontation such that a person accused of manslaughter or murder would have felt justified in using lethal force?

This is the question that investigators and prosecutors try to answer before any criminal charges are filed. This normally falls in the realm of self-defense, but on rare occasions, it may cross into the surreal.

There is a phrase that was once common in Texas and other parts of the South and Southwest: "He needed killing." Granted, in a court of law that is not going to equate to justification for taking as life, but the origin of this sentiment is an allusion to a decedent's behavior, not only immediately prior to being killed, but also overall in his life. Harsh as it may seem, there are some people whose overall pattern of behavior is so consistently threatening and frequently dangerous that their presence might constitute a threat to safety.

This might apply to career criminals; people who make a habit of making others' lives miserable. Being obnoxious is not a capital offense.

The single case that may provide some insight into how very bad such situations can ultimately turn out involved a man named Ken Rex McElroy, once described as the "town bully" of Skidmore, Missouri, and about whose unsolved slaying a book was published in 1988, and television movie was made in 1991 with the character given a fictional name.

According to a history of this remarkable case that was assembled by Wikipedia, McElroy was indicted 21 times, convicted only once, but accused of all manner of crimes from cattle rustling to statutory rape, arson and attempted murder. On July 10, 1981, he was fatally shot after appealing the one conviction in his life, for assault, for reportedly having shot and wounded a local grocer in 1980. After allegedly making threats against the man who had been shot, McElroy was sitting in his pickup truck when an unknown individual or individuals shot him, as he was struck by rounds from two different firearms.

There is nothing in SYG that allows for what amounts to a public execution, even involving someone as allegedly vile as McElroy. It would stretch credulity to claim self-defense or to even remotely suggest you were "standing your ground" to shoot someone from ambush, in cold blood.

This fellow, and the circumstances of his death, were described in the true crime book, *In Broad Daylight*, which won an Edgar Award for author Harry N. MacLean.

There does not appear to have been a case like McElroy's either before or in the decades since. A lengthy investigation by federal officials did not produce any criminal charges. There were more than 40 possible witnesses, but nobody could identify who fired the shots.

About three years later, McElroy's wife, Trena, filed a $6 million wrongful death lawsuit against the Town of Skidmore and Nodaway County, the sheriff, the town mayor and one individual she believed was one of the shooters, but who was not charged, according to the Wikipedia account. She reportedly settled for $17,600.

Vigilante justice is not justice at all, nor would it ever be protected by an SYG law. The right to carry is not a license to kill. Repeat that to yourself frequently. We use the McElroy story to illustrate an extreme situation that should hardly serve as an example of what might be done about neighborhood or small town trouble-makers. Indeed, it's more of an example of what *cannot* be done.

Nobody was standing his ground, within the accepted parameters of SYG, when McElroy was slain. His slayers shot him from ambush. There is no way one could even remotely suggest this was self-defense.

To answer the question posed at the start of this section, "he had it coming" will not provide a defense for anyone charged in the killing of another person, and claiming that you were standing your ground when you actually shoot someone from ambush won't get any traction at all.

Opposing Stand-Your-Ground

Perhaps nowhere has opposition to SYG been so crystalized than in Florida, primarily because of the Trayvon Martin case mentioned at the beginning of this chapter, but because of several other cases in that state as well. The left's angst over SYG even entered the presidential political arena when former Gov. Jeb Bush, who was in the large Republican field of candidates, became the target of what *The Blaze* called "Liberal groups favoring gun control."

When the law was passed with bipartisan support in the Florida legislature – the House passed it 94-20 and the Senate passed it 39-0 – apparently some people didn't understand the ramifications until citizens who used the law began claiming it as part of their defense strategy after they had shot someone. For many on the political left, the *concept* of self-defense is fine, but the *utilization* of self-defense – especially in cases where white people shoot black people – is a politically incorrect no-no.

Bush signed the law, but it wasn't as though he acted unilaterally. Only years later, when he was running as a Republican for president, against the likelihood of Hillary Rodham Clinton candidacy for the Democrats, the political left was out to destroy any threat to their anointed one.

The Blaze story noted a report from the liberal Center for American Progress that argued murders had climbed under SYG, but the murder rate had declined, according to Erich Pratt, a spokesman for the Gun Owners of America. The Center's Action Fund went so far as to dub SYG "Jeb Bush's License to Kill," according to a report in the *Miami Herald*. It was essentially political because the story came in advance of when the former governor was to give a speech before the National Urban League in Fort Lauderdale as part of his presidential campaign activities. With that group, SYG is a sensitive subject because of the Trayvon Martin case, and the newspaper reminded readers that "Urban League President Marc Morial, a Democrat and former New Orleans mayor, called stand your ground legislation 'kill at will laws' after Martin's death."

Writing for the *Daily Business Review*, Jill Kahn brought the issue into its proper perspective, in a story headlined appropriately "Confusion Reigns in Stand-Your-Ground Decisions." That is really the problem with SYG, at least as the average citizen understands the controversy after being bombarded by conflicting, and sometimes erroneous, discussions in the media.

Kahn's matter-of-fact piece focused on how judges could not even concur on how to enforce the SYG statute in Florida, because one of the jury instructions was "baffling," according to the defendant's attorney. One of the appeals court judges called the specific instruction "a repetitive, confusing morass."

Long story short, SYG as a defense quickly takes on a life of its own. It definitely is not a snap-your-fingers kind of law, at least as it is being enforced in the Sunshine State. But remember, SYG is relatively new legal territory in lots of places, even in Florida though the statute has been on the books for more than a decade. Proponents and opponents of such laws will use that to pick legal nits, with the citizen who claims he or she was standing their ground being stuck in the middle of what essentially becomes a game of one-upmanship as the courts sort through the arguments.

But there is more, and it involves the invocation of what is typically called an "affirmative defense." This is the proverbial "down side" of SYG, in that when it is invoked as a defense, the defendant – as noted in an editorial in the *Ocala Star-Banner* – "bears the burden of proof by a preponderance of the evidence at the pretrial evidentiary hearing."

Rather than requiring the state to prove one's guilt beyond a reasonable doubt, the defendant has to prove he/she is innocent, and thus be spared from prosecution. As the newspaper editorial put it, "the person who invokes Stand Your Ground in defense of his actions — bears the burden of proving a violent act was motivated by self-defense, and thus should be excused from prosecution."

The newspaper used the opportunity to suggest that the legislature revisit SYG, not necessarily to rewrite the law, but to "rework its language to be more definitive and to clarify who, exactly, is responsible for making the case about a justification of force." Would this be the solution that Florida courts, prosecutors and defense attorneys have needed almost since the law took effect? Maybe, and you can bet all the other states with similar statutes would pay close attention to how state lawmakers worked out this new language.

Meanwhile, it remains incumbent on the armed private citizen to be very careful about relying on SYG to get one's self out of a legal jam.

Lesson from the OK Corral

While we have discussed the philosophical and legal ramifications of SYG, let's take a quick look at the concept as seen through the eyes of some advocates, for whom the right to carry may provide armed citizens with the power to simply say they're "not taking any crap from anybody." That's not what SYG was ever intended for.

Like it or not, prisons are often home to people who once thought that way, and anti-gun prosecutors lick their chops at every opportunity to take such individuals to trial and make public examples of them.

Here's a question: Faced with what you conclude is imminent and possibly unavoidable danger of grave bodily harm or death, should you turn and run from that threat? This might go over just fine with the legions of anti-gunners who hate guns and the people who own them, and are afraid of fighting back. But it may not go over well with other individuals for whom retreat is never an option.

In the real world, there are problems with the strategy of turning one's back and running from an immediate threat. As noted near the beginning of this chapter, some self-defense experts maintain that turning and running offers a very vulnerable target for someone who could easily stab or shoot you in the back. Even without a knife or gun, an assailant could pursue and attack from behind, quickly overpower even an armed citizen and pummel them to the ground. Indeed, that is the scenario that appears to have unfolded between Martin and Zimmerman that dark night in Florida.

To illustrate, let's take a look at the infamous "Knock-out Game" that got plenty of notoriety a couple of years ago, and is still being reported from time to time, though not with as much attention or discussion on television news. The game, which appears to be popular among inner city teens with nothing better to do – in some places they're called "thugs" – will come from behind and viciously strike a man or woman to knock them out.

In 2013 in Lansing, Michigan, this foolishness nearly cost the perpetrator his life. Marvell Weaver did time behind bars after he recovered from gunshot wounds inflicted by the man he attacked. But the way it was described by Breitbart.com reveals what some might call a textbook example of justifiable self-defense and the use of force.

Weaver, who is black, attacked a man waiting at a bus stop for his daughter. That man was white. Weaver didn't just punch his intended victim, he tried to disable the man with a Taser, but the little tool malfunctioned. That's when Weaver got the most unpleasant, and nearly last, surprise of his young life.

The man he had attacked drew a legally-carried .40-caliber semi-auto pistol and shot Weaver twice. Weaver, who had admitted attacking about a half-dozen other people prior to the assault on the armed citizen, described what happened as "a lesson learned." That's not the best way to learn a lesson.

The right to carry brings with it the ability to use a firearm in self-defense, and a brutal attack in a public place will, under most self-defense statutes, justify a decisive response. A couple of these "knockout game" cases have left people dead, and a random attack in a public place would hardly be condoned by a rational jury.

While some self-defense statutes include a duty to retreat provision, showing that there must be an attempt to avoid a conflict, that typically falls by the wayside once an attack has commenced. At the famous "Gunfight at the OK Corral" in Tombstone, Arizona on Oct. 26, 1881, it has been fairly well documented that Wyatt Earp actually permitted one of the main opponents, Ike Clanton, to run away after the shooting started, telling him according to popular history, "The fight's commenced. Get to fighting or get away." Clanton was not armed when the shooting started. The gun battle has been meticulously detailed in many books and magazine articles, including Wikipedia. It has also been dramatically misrepresented in so many films as to be the stuff of myth.

Whether Earp actually said that to Clanton, there was already lead in the air and at least two of the combatants, Billy Clanton and Frank McLaury, had been shot, and the gunfight wasn't even finished, despite its total duration of only about 30 seconds. During that time, three of the people involved were killed or mortally wounded, two fled and three others were wounded, and at least 30 shots had been fired. The distance between combatants may have been as little as six feet, in an empty lot that was no more than 15 feet wide. There is not much room to maneuver, much less retreat, in such a tight space, especially with at least one horse present.

This case is used specifically to demonstrate that any duty to retreat immediately becomes a moot point once a violent attack has erupted. At that point, an attempted retreat could get one killed, if retreat is even possible at all. The fact that Ike Clanton was able to get away with all of the bullets flying around is nothing short of a miracle.

The duty to retreat concept might be designed show that there was a genuine attempt to avoid conflict before using force. Critics of the requirement are quick to observe that it does not take into account the viciousness of an intended attacker to actually inflict injury on a victim.

Also keep in mind that there was a legal aftermath of the Tombstone gunfight that was rarely seen in the movies. Wyatt Earp and his brothers, and their companion, John H. "Doc" Holliday, were all charged with murder and had to defend themselves in court. There was conflicting testimony, and there was physical evidence that helped exonerate the Earp faction from wrongdoing.

Today, there are vast improvements in the collection of evidence and mapping crime scenes, and there may even be digital recordings of self-defense incidents thanks to a growing use of security cameras in urban and even suburban environments. All of these advances can help prevent an unnecessary prosecution in a true self-defense/SYG case, or they can help send one to jail.

Homicides actually declined

As noted earlier in this chapter, critics of SYG laws maintain that their passage has actually increased the number of homicides annually around the United States by several hundred. According to a study published in the *Journal of Human Resources*, co-authored by Mark Hoestra (and referred to earlier in this chapter), there may be as many as 600 additional homicides in a given year due to SYG, according to a brief overview by *Global Grind*.

Naturally, that number is debatable. What does not appear to be in question is that the passage of these laws in about half of the states has enabled armed citizens to worry less about being prosecuted for acting in self-defense than using force at all. Under duty to retreat requirements, there is always the possibility that one could be prosecuted for acting in one's own defense or protecting someone else, regardless the strength of their justification.

Remember what happened to Zimmerman. There are many who believe his prosecution was strictly political in nature, and that all of the evidence from the investigation supported his version of the events. Others still use him as a symbol of irresponsibility.

A duty-to-retreat requirement is pretty close to forcing the intended victim of a crime to allow the perpetrator an unchallenged first strike, whether with a firearm, knife, club, brick, baseball bat; any potentially lethal weapon. It's almost as if criminals cooked up such laws.

Quoting Hoestra, the *Global Grind* story said the information about additional slayings was "sobering news."

Even so, FBI uniform crime data over the past several years has shown a steady decrease in the annual number of firearm-related homicides, although a report released in mid-2015 by the Congressional Research Service titled *Mass Murder with Firearms: Incidents and Victims, 1993-2013* indicated that the number of fatal mass shootings had increased slightly over the past few decades.

Where homicides once hovered about 10,000 annually, today the number lies somewhere between 8,000 and 9,000, and that's significant in a nation with some 200 million-plus firearms owned by tens of millions of citizens. If the United States were as bloody and dangerous as the gun prohibition lobby asserts, then the casualty count should be twice or even three times that number.

It may be during one of these mass-shooting incidents that the SYG principle becomes most valuable to an armed citizen. While under no legal obligation to protect others, there is a moral angle that every responsible armed citizen has at least once thought about: If you are in a position to utilize a defensive sidearm and stop a horrible crime in progress, should you do it?

There may be no right or wrong answer to that question. It is not as if you are assassinating an alleged town bully while he is sitting in a truck. If you suddenly find yourself in the middle of chaos – an active shooter situation – and you have an opportunity to take a clear shot with your legally-carried handgun, do you take the shot or do you retreat to cover with the potential that others might still be injured or killed? Which course of action do you take, because you will be living with that decision forever.

The right to carry does have emotional baggage. If you pull the trigger, your life will never be the same, regardless what keyboard heroes on the Internet forums might argue. If you don't press the trigger, and other innocents fall because you did nothing, do you carry a sense of guilt for the remainder of your days?

8: EDITORIAL BIAS

"There is something about the mainstream press that has always impressed us. At every turn, the current always seems to flow strongly toward the left bank." – Dave Workman

Combining elitism and an often painfully embarrassing lack of knowledge about firearms with an all-too-frequent sneering disdain or dismissiveness toward the Second Amendment has seemed to become a pattern among many people within the Fourth Estate.

Editorial writers at best begrudgingly acknowledge that the Second Amendment protects a right to keep and bear arms, but seem perennially inclined to support measures that seek to erode that civil right to the point of being little more than a heavily-regulated government privilege. One might be inclined to suspect that if an editorial were discussing any other of the individual rights delineated and protected by the Bill of Rights – and especially the First Amendment – there would be righteous indignation in every syllable against anything remotely threatening the sanctity of that right.

Even in the news columns one cannot get away from sensing a down-the-nose view of gun owners by journalists. A sterling example came when a mom and former Marine from Texas was arrested in New York City for carrying two concealed handguns at the Ground Zero memorial.

While it is, or at least should be, widely known that New York gun laws are among the strictest, and most draconian, in the nation, the way the *New York Post* reported the story smacked of cultural bigotry.

They reported that the suspect in this case, Elizabeth Anne Enderli, was "treating the 9/11 memorial like an Old West saloon." This seemed to be a reference to what many people have been led to believe about the Old West, largely by Hollywood, that cowboys and gunslingers checked their hardware with the barkeep when they entered a saloon.

This wasn't the first time that newspaper actually used that caricature in a story about some armed tourist being pinched with a gun at the 9/11 memorial. Almost two years earlier, in September 2013, a visitor from Milwaukee got into the same trouble, only that time, the *Post* wrote, "Another dopey tourist was caught at Ground Zero Sunday, traipsing into the 9/11 Memorial with a handgun, law-enforcement sources said...Ursula Jerry, 41, of Milwaukee never got past the guards... Jerry isn't the first hick from the sticks to treat the WTC — and the city in general — site like an Old West saloon."

Well, not everyone can be as sophisticated as the editorial staff at the New York Post, but since gun owners represent a fairly diverse cross-section of the population – including doctors, attorneys, judges, teachers, housewives, engineers, airline pilots, veterinarians, writers, mechanics, electricians and so forth from all ethnic and religious backgrounds – it seems a rather broad brush slap at people who live in other states where they still can enjoy firearms freedom and not be treated like criminals or bumpkins.

In a revealing look at how the Big Three networks covered President Barack Obama's efforts to push his gun control agenda in the weeks following the 2012 attack at Sandy Hook Elementary in Newtown, Connecticut, the Media Research Center (MRC) analyzed 216 gun policy stories broadcast by ABC, CBS and NBC, and found rather lopsided coverage. The MRC concluded that the networks "quickly moved to exploit the tragedy to push for more gun control legislation while mostly ignoring solutions that respect gun owners' Second Amendment rights."

The center further reported that there was an 8-to-1 imbalance between stories advocating for more gun control laws than those opposing new gun restrictions. Additionally, MRC noted that "Anti-gun soundbites were aired almost twice as frequently than (sic) pro-gun ones (228 to 134)."

If this is surprising to anyone, it shouldn't be. There has been a long-standing, albeit sometimes subtle, media effort to denigrate the Second Amendment, guns and the people who own them. While recent reporting at some local and even regional news agencies shows some effort at improving and offering more balance, it isn't always the case.

Even more disturbing to those paying attention to the coverage of "the gun issue" following Sandy Hook was the fact that "Gun control advocates appeared as guests on 26 occasions, compared to 7 times for gun rights advocates. CBS was the most stridently anti-gun rights network. By a whopping 22 to 1 ratio, CBS aired more stories that favored gun control (44) to those that supported gun rights (2), with 37 neutral pieces. ABC aired almost six times as many stories that favored gun control (29) to those that favored gun rights, with 25 neutral stories. NBC pushed for more gun control in 26 of their stories to just 5 that tilted in favor of gun rights for a 5 to 1 ratio, with 43 neutral segments."

According to the MRC report, there had been very little change between media coverage patterns following Sandy Hook and how the press covered the aftermath of the Columbine High School tragedy several years earlier.

The bottom line in the MRC report was detailed in three short bullet points:

- CBS's *Evening News* was the most biased in favor of gun control, airing 19 anti-gun stories to only 1 pro-gun segment, with 20 neutral stories. Anti-gun talking heads (42) outnumbered pro-gun talking heads (21) by a 2 to 1 ratio, with 17 neutral soundbites.

- ABC's *World News* wasn't much better, airing 15 anti-gun segments to just 2 pro-gun segments, with 8 neutral stories. Surprisingly, ABC's World News did offer a fairer result when it came to soundbites as anti-talking heads (28) almost matched pro-talking heads (27) with 15 being neutral.

- NBC's *Nightly News* offered 12 anti-gun segments and delivered 3 pro-gun segments, with 12 neutral stories. On *Nightly News*, 51 talking heads supported gun control to just 29 opposed to more regulations, 20 soundbites were neutral.

MRC called this a "staggering imbalance," and there is no reason to contest that conclusion. Granted, as noted above, the mainstream press has been improving at times with its coverage of gun issues, but not always.

There was a time when reporters would simply try to work in the "obligatory remark of disagreement" just to claim balance, but today there does appear to be a stronger effort to get a Second Amendment viewpoint into the conversation, and more prominently.

Part of this may be due to the influence of cable network news, notably Fox News, and the internet. Online eyewitness reports have become a counter to network news domination, and people no longer have to get their news only from networks and affiliates.

Whether one cares for Fox News on the whole, or otherwise, it must be noted that the leading cable news network has been far more balanced in its coverage of gun-related news, so much so that Fox critics see them as "pro-gun." That may not be accurate. Perhaps they are merely telling both sides of a story.

Gun owners 'dig in'

When the *Boston Globe* published a piece on gun control that focused on the National Rifle Association's Colion Noir – a rather effective African-American firearms enthusiast with a knack for calling out anti-gunners on their false narratives – it quoted Matt Grossman, a Michigan State University political science professor, who advised against demonizing gun owners, because that only makes them "dig in." Experience has taught just about everyone that lesson, because it has been widely held that the so-called "gun lobby," which consists of millions of Second Amendment activists, fights most effectively from behind circled wagons.

The mainstream press probably never set out to be known as "the anti-gun media," but that is certainly how reporters, editorial writers and broadcast journalists are perceived by a majority of gun owners. The Boston Globe's piece seemed to lament over the fact that a 1999 survey of gun owners, it found that 49 percent owned firearms for hunting and only 26 percent had them for personal protection.

However, a 2013 Pew Research Center survey revealed an astounding reversal in public sentiment. Forty-eight percent of the survey respondents had guns for personal protection while 32 percent had guns for hunting.

It should come as no surprise that with the growing number of people who have purchased guns for self-defense there has been an accompanying surge in the number of applications for concealed carry permits and licenses. Not only have these citizens decided to exercise their right to *keep* arms, they want to *bear* them as well!

Let's look at just one state as an example of this phenomenon: Washington. The authors have been tracking the steady rise in concealed pistol licenses in the Evergreen State for more than two years. In January 2013, that state's Department of Licensing reported that there were 392,784 active CPLs, which placed it among the Top Ten – where it has consistently been for many years – of *per capita* concealed carry.

What's up with this? Washington has voted pretty consistently for Democrat presidents and U.S. Senators for several years, yet despite the predominance of liberal-leaning voters in the Seattle and Puget Sound area, gun ownership is something the self-appointed "progressives" have yet been able to stamp out.

Leap ahead to January 2014 and we see there were 449,532 active CPLs reported, an increase of 56,748 licenses in a "blue" state over the course of 12 months. That's more than 4,700 new licenses each month, which is more than some states issue in a year.

In January 2015, things had slowed down, with only 29,052 new licenses for the previous year, bringing the number to 478,584 total active CPLs. However, the number continued to surge toward the half-million mark.

But the mainstream press, including the award-winning *Seattle Times* and the network affiliates for ABC, NBC, CBS and even FOX seemed to religiously avoid reporting this steady increase in the number of legally-armed citizens. It is as though the press decided this was not important news, and perhaps they are right if one considers that it is nobody's business, and certainly not the government's business, who has a gun and why.

The Bias Against Guns

In his 2003 book *The Bias Against Guns*, author John Lott notes at the beginning of the final chapter, "The debate on gun control would be very different if even a few defensive gun use cases were covered better in the news. Too often, the debate over guns is a philosophical one, pitting the freedom of gun owners against the safety of everyone else."

Lott devoted an entire chapter to how the media handles firearms stories, and it is not terribly flattering. He noted that a 1985 survey of some 3,000 journalists by the *Los Angeles Times* revealed "that while only half of the public supported stricter handgun controls, 78 percent of journalists wanted more regulations." Lott added a caveat of sorts, explaining that he was not asserting the survey results explained "the vast majority of decisions behind what gun stories the media decide to cover."

There is something of an unwritten axiom that seems to apply to news and how it is reported. "If it bleeds," according to the questionable principle, which nobody in journalism will ever acknowledge as fact-based, "it leads." That may be all Hollywood, but it also applies to something that most journalists have been learning for years. If a story is compelling and dramatic, if it grabs the reader/viewer attention and holds it, that's "news."

If something doesn't happen, that's not newsworthy at all. Nobody is going to headline a story on the front page or the top of the hour about, say, kids playing in a park without incident.

But in his chapter about media bias, Lott discusses the famous Appalachian Law School shooting in 2002. Rarely was it reported that two armed students intervened in that event and the attack was stopped. Instead, a Nexis-Lexis search revealed to Lott that "in the week after the event, just four stories mentioned that the students who stopped the attack had guns." That was out of 208 total stories about the shooting that he found during the computer search.

That's bias by omission, and Lott's narrative told how one of the nation's leading newspapers virtually ignored the fact that two students had retrieved guns from their cars and stopped the shooter. Instead, the published story reported that the gunman was restrained by other students.

When CNS News interviewed Lott in 2008 for a story headlined "Author Accuses Media of Intentional Bias Against Guns," the writer touched on details about news coverage in various major newspapers, with the negative outweighing the positive.

But is there really an *intentional* bias against firearms? Another veteran researcher and gun rights author, David Kopel, isn't convinced. He published an essay headlined "Media Bias in Coverage of Gun Control" on his own website, and he insisted, "While it is easy for critics of the media to point out inaccuracies in individual stories, proving more systematic bias is difficult."

"The notion that the American press is monolithically liberal, or monolithically anti-gun, is quite wrong," Kopel asserted.

But then came this acknowledgement: "Of course most of the newspapers that make up the conservative majority of the press are small town papers…"

Is Kopel being disingenuous? No, not really, though some people might make that presumption. He's putting the contention that the press is uniformly anti-gun into a perspective that many people never consider. There are more small-town newspapers than major city newspapers, and those small town publications tend to reflect the values of their communities. However, one might argue that it is editorial opinion in the larger newspapers that gets more attention, and tends to influence more voters, and certainly more state-level politicians.

One simply cannot broad brush the press and declare the whole lot of journalists to be anti-gun shills. It doesn't work that way and never has. At times it seems as though every newspaper editor in the country is a card-carrying supporter of the Brady Campaign, but that's as unfair an assessment as a lopsided editorial calling for a ban on handguns because some people misuse them.

Gun bias workshop

The mainstream press does itself no favors, of course, when it allows itself to be played into a scenario that suggests there is an anti-gun philosophy that dominates news decisions. No better example of this was attendance at a workshop sponsored by the Dart Center for Journalism and Trauma in Phoenix, Arizona that received support from anti-gun billionaire Michael Bloomberg's "Everytown for Gun Safety."

The Dart Center for Journalism is a project of the Columbia University Graduate School of Journalism, and one might easily argue that the university could have told Bloomberg's group to keep its money. The whole thing smelled of bias among Second Amendment activists, especially after they read on-line how this two-day seminar was advertised.

"Reporting on gun violence – on individual incidents, policy shifts and polarized political debate – is a major challenge for journalists and news organizations," the promotion explained. "Every day, 86 Americans die of firearm related injuries, including nearly 12,000 murdered with guns each year – a rate 20 times higher than that of other developed countries. Nearly 100 school shootings have occurred since the massacre at Sandy Hook Elementary only two years ago."

But wait. According to the FBI Uniform Crime Statistics, there are fewer than 9,000 firearm-related murders annually, and that's been the case dating back to 2009. It has been much longer than that where more than 10,000 people have been murdered with firearms.

The event's goal was a lofty one: "Serve as a forum for improving journalists' knowledge of guns and gun violence, and the implications of public policies like background check requirements."

Not surprisingly, Second Amendment activist organizations were highly critical of the workshop. In a bulletin to its members and associates, the Buckeye Firearms Organization in Ohio (BFO) veteran gun rights advocate Jeff Knox observed, with no small amount of sarcasm, "Surely the Dart Center, a project of the Columbia University Graduate School of Journalism could help improve the state of reporting on the firearms issue, especially in light of the way reporters seem to call every pistol a Glock, every rifle an AK47, and every gun an automatic."

Later in his column, Knox wrote, "Perhaps I'm wrong, but while I have no doubt there will be much said in this workshop about the horrors of 'gun violence,' and the common sense of 'universal background checks,' I would be very surprised to learn that there was anything presented about the positive benefits of gun ownership or the arguments against Bloomberg's backdoor registration scheme."

Media 'watchdogs' bite

There are a couple of media watchdog groups that carefully monitor the left-leaning mainstream press, and when it comes to guns, Newsbusters' Geoffrey Dickens did a blistering piece in May 2013 that could easily be used today to show an existing bias. In a piece headlined "The Power of Media Bias: Most Americans Wrongly Believe Gun Violence Has Increased," Dickens showed how news coverage of violent events had apparently convinced the public that crime was on the rise, while the results of a Pew Research Center poll revealed clearly the opposite was true.

At that time, he noted, "The extent of the media's influence to shape public opinion was on full display in a new Pew Research Center poll that shows, even though gun crime has dropped by half since its peak in the mid '90s, most Americans (56 percent) wrongly think gun violence has increased."

The story explained how the Media Research Center discovered that after the Newtown tragedy of December 2012, media coverage had been "driving the misconception" that violent crime was up when it was actually down. Gun-related homicides had declined a stunning 39 percent between 1913 and 2011, but more than half the population, according to a Pew poll, thought violence had increased.

Where statistics show that violence has declined, there are always newspaper editorials ready to predict that some sensible gun law reform will make it surge. That could easily be said about an editorial in the *Missoulian*, a Montana newspaper that editorialized against legislation that would allow the possession of firearms on university property in the state.

When the newspaper urged readers to oppose the measure, it wrote, "Just as it makes sense to prohibit firearms from county detention centers and federal courthouses, it makes sense to prohibit them from campus. Most reasonable people agree that guns, like alcohol, do not belong in every public square. They do not belong at sporting events, school rallies or graduation ceremonies. It's a simple matter of safety.

"Campus security has its hands full already policing underage alcohol consumption and intoxication," the newspaper said. "Adding guns to the mix seems like a recipe for tragedy."

If the emotional appeal doesn't work, there's always the financial aspect, and the *Missoulian* editorial went there as well, asserting, "Furthermore, concealed carry is bound to be hugely expensive for our tightly budgeted institutions of higher learning. The *Idaho Statesman* reported just this month that a handful of colleges and universities in that state spent more than $1.5 million on security measures after a law passed allowed concealed carry. The schools estimated that the total cost would exceed $3.7 million in the first year."

That kind of approach is designed to hit conservatives with their own sensitivity about money. As an old-timer once observed, the thing a conservative is *most* conservative about is a dollar.

Raising false alarms?

When the West Virginia legislature was considering a "constitutional carry" measure in 2015 to eliminate the need for a concealed carry permit, newspaper editorials went all out against the proposal. The *Herald-Dispatch* in Huntington raised alarms that people would be able to legally carry a concealed sidearm and "no longer be subject to the background checks or taking the gun safety training." As noted earlier, one year later, the Legislature overrode the governor's second veto of such legislation.

The concern seemed to be that government regulation of a civil right would be eroded. As if to paint all would-be armed citizens into the same corner, the editorial observed, "Currently, state law requires that people 21 or older who want to carry a concealed handgun must apply for a permit with the sheriff in the county where they reside. The sheriff will conduct a background check to determine whether the individual's history would disqualify him or her from having a permit. The background check looks for evidence of alcohol or drug addiction, convictions for driving under the influence, any felony convictions, domestic violence convictions, current indictments, mental incompetence or any prohibitions for carrying a weapon under federal law."

The newspaper also noted that training was mandatory for getting a permit under the existing law.

"But eliminating the requirements," the newspaper maintained, "opens the possibility for many people to avoid the background checks. While purchasing a gun from a federally licensed dealer requires a background check at the federal level, the tens of thousands of guns purchased at gun shows or between private parties across the nation are not subject to the federal background checks. Eliminating the state's concealed carry permit requirement also means another layer of protection is removed."

No, what it meant was that another layer of bureaucracy would be removed from the process through which citizens had to travel in order to bear arms. Newspapers are big on background checks when it comes to firearms.

No law-abiding gun owner wants would-be terrorists, criminals or crazy people to carry firearms or even possess them. Restricting the ability of honest citizens to exercise their Second Amendment rights is not, nor has it ever, prevented an outlaw or determined psychopath from getting his or her hands on a weapon with which they have done harm.

As noted earlier in this book, the West Virginia legislation was ultimately vetoed despite strong support in the legislature, but one year later, after a similar bill was passed and the governor vetoed it a second time, state lawmakers overrode that veto.

In 2015, Mountain State editorial writers opposed to the legislation chalked the veto up as a victory, but it might just as easily have been called a loss for civil rights that infuriated lawmakers, and they came back a year later to square accounts.

Once you establish that government can regulate the right to bear arms beyond the common-sense level of manner, time and place (i.e., strolling down the middle of a shopping mall with an AR-15 held at "low ready") then government is going to try to grab more authority incrementally, and newspapers that support any manner of gun control will be right there to cheer them on.

9: GOVERNMENT DEMAGOGUERY

"Council President Kevin Kelley said that the legislation was not designed to stop gun violence. Rather, it is a reflection of council's values and is good public policy intended to encourage responsible gun ownership, he said." — Cleveland Plain Dealer

When the city council in Cleveland, Ohio adopted what was described by one news blogger as "a sweeping body of gun control measures" in April 2015, the justification by Council President Kevin Kelley was astonishing, if not downright appalling.

He essentially acknowledged that the measures were symbolism over substance, a common thread among gun control legislation and the people who support and push it.

Gun control proponents would never admit that what they sell is essentially political snake oil. They want the public to believe they have accomplished something when in reality, they may have accomplished less than nothing. It amounts to showmanship and the need for what has become known as "trophy legislation."

Certainly, no politician is going to admit that he or she has just handed their constituents a shovel full of fecal matter and claimed it was chocolate pudding. Instead, they force-feed it to the voters in the form of a mandate, with penalties for not taking a mouthful and swallowing.

The *Cleveland Plain Dealer* noted that the legislation carried a lot of requirements – none of which would have prevented any of the 25 homicides committed so far that year, according to the single council critic, Councilman Zack Reed – that put the law squarely on the shoulders of law-abiding gun owners in the city, but not the criminals who were committing gun-related crimes.

Among the requirements were safe storage, reporting of private gun sales to police, reporting of lost or stolen firearms, and it created something called a "gun offender registry" consisting of the names of people convicted of so-called "gun crimes."

One of the state's leading gun rights organizations, Ohioans for Concealed Carry, promptly filed a lawsuit. The group maintained that the new ordinances violated what has generically become known as the Buckeye State's preemption statute. This and similar laws adopted by state legislatures all over the country place firearms regulation solely in the hands of said legislatures and prohibit cities, towns and counties from adopting more stringent regulations.

Breitbart's AWR Hawkins, commenting on the new regulations, posed a question nobody answered: "Does this mean criminals and gang members will no longer sell or transfer guns without talking to police, or is it really just another law that will burden law-abiding citizens?"

None of these local ordinances has ever been proven to have prevented a single crime. But they make a big impression with the low-information municipal voter who may not like guns, and when the goal is flash rather than substance, that's what counts.

This is the same kind of mentality that guided a proposed ban on firearms in city park property by the City of Seattle back in 2009. Then-Mayor Greg Nickels, a founding member of Michael Bloomberg's Mayors Against Illegal Guns, pushed the ban as an administrative rule rather than an ordinance in a too-clever-by-half attempt to skirt the state preemption law, but the courts didn't buy it. A lawsuit by several leading gun rights groups including the Second Amendment Foundation and National Rifle Association went against the city at trial and in the State Court of Appeals. When the city tried to take it to the state Supreme Court, the high court flatly turned the case down for review.

Had it prevailed, the city parks gun ban would not have prevented a single crime, but municipal government demagogues don't really care about that. This isn't about *protecting* people, it's about *controlling* them.

To paraphrase the late Charlton Heston, when you think something will work and it doesn't, that's a mistake, but when you know something won't work and you do it anyway, that's stupid. Some might even dare to call it malfeasance, but a more appropriate word might just be fraud.

When it filed the lawsuit, Ohioans for Concealed Carry dubbed the Cleveland measures as a "decoy issue." In many cases that would be an appropriate definition because such issues divert public attention away from the real problem, and onto a manufactured one. In the end, such laws might even be said to do less than nothing by wasting energy on the decoy issues while the real problems continue to fester.

'Calling B.S.' in Oregon

During its 2015 session, the Democrat-dominated Oregon Legislature adopted Senate Bill 941, a so-called "universal background check" measure patterned after a law passed by voters in neighboring Washington the previous November. Proponents of both the Evergreen State initiative and the Beaver State legislation were careful to couch their words by creating the impression that such checks – to include the loans or gifting of firearms with a few narrow and specific exemptions – would have some sort of impact on crime, including domestic violence.

Remarkably, the most spirited opposition to the measure came from Democrat State Senator Betsy Johnson, who published Op-ed pieces in a couple of influential newspapers, including the *Portland Oregonian*. Johnson effectively – albeit not effectively enough to prevent SB 941 from becoming law – lambasted the legislation and exposed it for what it really was: Feel-good legislation that will not impact criminals, but will definitely inconvenience, and perhaps even criminalize, common behavior among law-abiding citizens that has never created a problem for anybody.

Said Johnson in her *Oregonian* piece: "What everybody wants, though, is to keep guns out of the wrong hands. There is no law that can do that. None. Even outright confiscation and a ban won't keep guns out of the wrong hands. Any politician who tells you otherwise is either lying or desperate to look like he or she is doing something. The brutal truth is that too many of my colleagues don't want to acknowledge that mistakes have been made."

It is a rare politician who calls B.S. on members of her own party. But Johnson was rather good at it.

"Ex-felons already know they cannot legally possess a gun unless they successfully petition the court," the senator noted. "Not surprisingly, most ex-felons who acquire a gun do so on the black market or through other illegal means. SB941 won't change that. As for halting gun sales to the mentally ill, that is a noble cause. Unfortunately, many of the mentally ill shooters who make the news are deemed mentally ill only after they kill someone."

But Johnson wasn't finished. She also carried the fight to the pages of the *Tillamook County Pioneer*. Declaring that the 2015 legislative session was "shaping up to be one of contradictions," she told readers of that newspaper that the strategy amounted to "more gun control for those who obey the law but possibly more government protection for those who have broken the law."

"We're about to increase background checks on private gun sales, which will do nothing to stop felons from continuing to illegally obtain and use firearms," Johnson explained. "At the same time, legislation has been proposed that would make it harder for an employer to do a criminal background check on felons."

Perhaps she summed up the problem among grandstanding liberal lawmakers who look more for the headlines than the headway against crime when she observed, "It takes more than laws to disarm a criminal."

Not that it matters, but gun control proponents seem prone to dance around any effort to make them provide evidence to prove "universal" background checks have prevented determined criminals from getting their hands on firearms illicitly. The typical fallback response does something like this: "Well, nobody can guarantee that this will prevent all cases of felons getting guns, but it's a step in the right direction."

It is nonsensical to presume that any kind of gun control law keeps guns out of the wrong hands, because one stroll through Chicago's South Side, or some neighborhoods in Detroit, East Los Angeles, Seattle's Rainier Valley, Maryland, Newark or just about any other city will provide convincing evidence to the contrary.

Teenage hoodlums manage to get firearms regularly, despite the strictness of local gun laws. That's because they learn at an early age that gun control laws don't affect them.

Of course, this is of no concern to the anti-gun politician who only wants to pass "one more law" as a trophy, even when he or she knows that the new law will not prevent a crime.

They know there's a problem

It is bad enough when elected officials adopt some new ordinance that results in restriction or confusion about a law, but worse when those officials know there is a problem, yet repeatedly do nothing about a solution. A case in point was the court fight between the city commission in Tallahassee, Florida and the Second Amendment Foundation and Florida Carry.

The two gun rights groups in May 2014 filed a lawsuit against the city because of a conflict with the state's preemption statute and gun control measures passed years before preemption became law. The city had been advised of the problem, yet the administration declined to fix it.

This resulted in a move against the city, a former mayor and a current mayor and members of the commission about 15 months later, by attorneys for SAF and Florida Carry. This appeared to be no accident or simple case of omission by the commission, but a deliberate effort to not change the ordinances to comply with the state law.

The attorneys for SAF and Florida Carry went to court in August 2015 to ask the judge to issue fines to the mayor and two members of the commission, and a former mayor. SAF's Alan Gottlieb, co-author of this book, wanted the officials to be dinged $5,000 apiece.

At the time, Gottlieb observed, "When public officials essentially ignore their responsibility to comply with the law, then they should be penalized in a way that gets their attention. A hefty fine that they can't pass on to the taxpayers is a good way to make that happen."

Nothing gets a politician's attention like being ordered by a judge to dig into his or her own wallet.

Another preemption case erupted in Seattle, Washington as this book was being written. The far left liberal city council, led by Council President Tim Burgess, unanimously passed a so-called "gun violence tax" on gun and ammunition retail sales, to raise what they expected to be between $300,000 and $500,000 to finance gun control research programs. Critics publicly doubted that the city would ever realize anything close to that amount of money, instead raising the possibility of a negative financial impact by the loss of those very businesses, and all of their sales tax revenues.

This tax was closely patterned after a similar measure adopted in Cook County, Illinois in 2013. That proposal was also designed to raise money for Chicago's gun control efforts, but it hardly stopped the violence that has plagued that city. In 2014, the city logged 434 homicides, which was up from the 415 in 2013, a year when the city reported the fewest slayings since 1965.

That's not a good example to follow if reducing homicides is the goal, but Seattle, with its unusually low murder rate for a city of its size, evidently figured to break the pattern. Several days after the city council okayed the gun and ammunition taxes, Mayor Ed Murray signed the measure into law.

Almost immediately, the Second Amendment Foundation, National Rifle Association and National Shooting Sports Foundation – the latter being the firearms industry organization – filed a legal challenge in King County Superior Court in Seattle, challenging the tax on state preemption grounds. Unlike Illinois, Washington State has a preemption law that prohibits cities, towns and counties from adopting their own gun control regulations, and the plaintiffs saw the new tax as a form of economic gun control.

One telling remark about Seattle's philosophy toward the then-32-year-old preemption statute came from veteran City Councilman Bruce Harrell in a campaign remark he made about crime and public safety in the pages of the Seattle Times. His comment did not go without notice.

"Seattle must be free to impose reasonable gun safety laws," Harrell said. "Therefore I will lead efforts to advocate for Seattle to be out from under the state pre-emption of gun laws as mandated by [the state law]."

There had been no small amount of conjecture that the attempt to pass the gun and ammunition sales tax was another test to see whether the city could whittle away at the state preemption law prior to Harrell's public statement. His comment tended to confirm for many in the firearms community what they had been theorizing.

As mentioned earlier in this chapter, this was not the first attempt by Seattle's liberal government establishment to test the preemption law. But it opened the door for a historic first with the lawsuit being filed jointly by SAF, NRA and NSSF.

Deliberately discouraging rules

For an adventure into the labyrinth of Draconian gun control, one need look no farther than Washington, D.C. The well-publicized adventures of author/journalist Emily Miller in her quest to get a permit to have a handgun in the District of Columbia merely for home protection became the basis for a series of columns in the *Washington Times* and ultimately a hardcover book titled *Emily Gets Her Gun...But Obama Wants to Take Yours*.

Both of these book's authors played small roles of support and assistance to Miller in the production of her book, which detailed what started as simply an effort and ended as a searing investigation of gun laws deliberately gone wrong through cost, some contradiction and no small amount of bureaucracy.

Many credit her dogged pursuit of a permit to own a handgun – and the discoveries she made along the way that became something of an embarrassment to official Washington when the red tape was completely disclosed – for exposing the city's gun policies that have resulted in lawsuits. She may not have earned friends at city hall, but she earned respect and admiration from Second Amendment activists all over the map.

Later, when Miller went through the process of obtaining one of the handful of carry permits, which were forced by a court ruling in *Palmer v. District of Columbia*, a case brought by the Second Amendment Foundation, Fox News, for which Miller was by then working at Fox affiliate WTTG as the chief investigative reporter, did a story on that as well.

Miller is a petite, determined – some say feisty – woman with a talent for asking the tough questions, and then questioning the answers.

The District's requirements for securing a carry permit were so demanding that they brought a second SAF lawsuit, this one challenging the regulatory scheme. The case is known as *Wrenn v. District of Columbia.*

During an interview with Fox News about her personal travails, she explained the miniscule number of carry permits matter-of-factly: "I guess because the hurdle is so high, people just aren't going through it."

No doubt that is by design. Municipalities with left liberal power structures dislike the idea of armed private citizens on their streets. They will seemingly go to any length to make the process discouraging if not unbearable, which explains in small part the desire by politicians in Seattle, mentioned earlier, to exempt that city from Washington State's preemption law.

Of course, Miller is not without her critics. The liberal website Media Matters claimed, in a critique of her book, that Miller was less than factual when she asserted that President Obama wanted to take guns. Insisting that, "Obama's Post-Newtown Proposals Did Not Involve Confiscation Or A National Gun Registry" and that the "Obama Administration Did Not Propose

Creation Of Registry Or Confiscation Of Firearms," Media Matters then virtually corrected itself by noting that Obama's post-Newtown plan included "Banning military-style assault weapons and high-capacity magazines..."

If firearms are banned, what are the owners supposed to do with them? Turn them in to the authorities, perhaps? That's "taking" by means of prohibition, and Media Matters knows it. But according to the blog, this ban was one of four "common-sense" (a term tossed out by the gun prohibition lobby as if to relegate any disagreement as nonsense or counter to common sense) steps "we can take right now."

The Garden of Evil

New Jersey calls itself "The Garden State," but if one were to ask the average gun owner, they might suggest that it's really a garden of evil; filled with weeds and tall grass in which predatory police and prosecutors lay in wait for careless law-abiding citizens. This state is something of a gulag when it comes to gun ownership, and gun owners are routinely treated like criminals. On more than one occasion, they have been turned into criminals for doing things that are legal just about anywhere else in the country.

There are so many gun rights horror stories from this state that it is difficult to pin down one or two and call them the worst. However, the saga of Shaneen Allen, a single African-American mom who was arrested and jailed in October 2013 for having her handgun and Pennsylvania concealed carry permit when she was pulled over on a traffic stop after crossing into the state, is an example of just how far a state can slide when demagoguery replaces common sense.

Allen, a resident of south Philadelphia, had gone through all of the necessary hoops to obtain a Pennsylvania carry permit. She had driven into New Jersey's Hamilton County enroute to a party when she was pulled over.

Being entirely honest, Allen revealed to the state trooper that she had her legally-licensed handgun and Pennsylvania carry permit. But this was in New Jersey, which does not recognize any other state's permit, and instead of spending a few hours with friends, she would spend many days in jail.

She was allowed to enter what the state calls a "pretrial program" for nonviolent offenders, and ultimately she applied for, and was granted, clemency by Gov. Chris Christie. Eager to telegraph to gun rights activists that he was a strong Second Amendment presidential candidate, the governor didn't simply commute her sentence, he issued a full and free pardon following a state parole board investigation.

Allen's case was hardly an aberration. Indeed, it is the sort of thing that has happened all too frequently in New Jersey. And Allen showed more than just spunk during her ordeal, which should send a signal to lawmakers in Trenton that their state statutes on firearms are in serious need of review and reform.

As noted by the *Philadelphia Inquirer*, when Allen was offered a plea bargain, she refused to take the deal. Represented by veteran Second Amendment attorney Evan Nappen, she was then offered the intervention program option. It just might be that public pressure helped bring that about, and when Christie pardoned her, that was the prize.

There are other horror stories about New Jersey gun laws and the heavy-handed way in which they are enforced. One that reaches toward the level set by Shaneen Allen's case involved a 72-year-old retired teacher in Maurice River Township. In early 2015, Gordon Van Gilder was being chauffeured around by 21-year-old Adam Puttergill. They had retrieved a 300-year-old flintlock pistol from a pawn shop and they were motoring though Cumberland County when their car was pulled over by a sheriff's deputy.

By no small coincidence, Nappen was also the defense attorney in this case. As the case unfolded, according to the story published by the *South Jersey Times* on NJ.com, the sheriff's department claimed that Van Gilder had advised deputies about the antique pistol, but also allegedly said the pair were in this particular neighborhood to buy drugs. But Van Gilder and Nappen denied that allegation, though Puttergill was charged for possession of a "controlled dangerous substance."

But charging a septuagenarian with a gun violation for having a 300-year-old flintlock pistol seemed just a bit over the top. The story ignited a national furor among conservatives and gun owners for the silliness of the charge. It did not take long before the prosecutor decided to drop the case against the older man.

Just to show how widely separated political affiliations are on the gun issue, here's what the *South Jersey Times* reported about the aftermath:

"Assemblywoman Caroline Casagrande (R-Monmouth) has said that she plans to introduce a bill that would align the state's law with a federal statute that exempts firearms manufactured before 1898."

"State Senator Jeff Van Drew (D-Cape May, Atlantic, Cumberland) has called for a bill that would allow a person convicted of unlawful possession admittance to pretrial intervention of supervisory treatment if they had no known association with a criminal street gang and no criminal convictions."

One wants to prevent criminal prosecutions altogether. The other seems okay with prosecution, allowing only a very narrow window for possible "supervisory treatment."

The leading demagogues

One cannot discuss anti-gun government demagoguery without mentioning the biggest anti-gun demagogue of them all, Senator Charles Schumer (D-NY). Naturally, there have been others vying for the spot including Sen. Dianne Feinstein (D-CA), New York Gov. Andrew Cuomo, and the late New Jersey Sen. Frank Lautenberg, but Schumer deserves recognition for a lifetime of devotion to the cause of gun control.

Since his days as a member of the House of Representatives, Schumer has never encountered a gun control measure he didn't champion or support. He voted for the ban on so-called "assault weapons." He was for waiting periods and background checks. He voted against the law that prevents harassment lawsuits against gun manufacturers. He wanted magazines banned. The list goes on…and on.

Chuck Schumer wanted to tinker with gun laws to find another way to deny someone his or her Second Amendment rights by pushing a requirement that the names of would-be gun buyers be "cross-referenced" through the Department of Homeland Security in an effort to prevent a gun sale to someone whose name appears on the so-called "no fly list" or a list of domestic terrorists.

But as *Western Journalism* called him out on the ploy in a story headlined "NY Senator Chuck Schumer's latest attempt at back door gun control." Author Tim Powers wrote the opinion piece and he didn't pull punches.

Complaining that he "would really like to know who the people are inside the federal government who determine who to classify as domestic terrorists and what their political affiliation is," Powers had an unnerving observation. Many of the people who might find themselves thus classified were returning veterans; people who had been overseas in combat zones. That little disclosure caused an uproar back in 2009 when then-DHS Secretary Janet Napolitano released the list of people who need watching, especially if they enter a gun store.

Schumer, and his anti-gun contemporaries will do anything to disqualify someone from exercising his or her Second Amendment right to keep and bear arms. He may profess to "support the Second Amendment," but his actions have consistently messaged to the public that he just doesn't believe anyone should actually exercise their gun rights.

In mid-2015, Schumer was in the headlines again – there is a standing joke on Capitol Hill that one should never get between Schumer and a television camera – the senator was at it again, this time with his cousin, comedian/actress Amy Schumer. This was in the aftermath of a theater shooting incident in which the film playing at the time was Miss Schumer's Trainwreck. It was what Reason called "a rewarmed serving of gun control proposals that the lawmaker has been trying to inflict on the American public for years." That was putting it mildly.

What the Schumers were after was the inclusion of increasing amounts of mental health information in the NICS system. Sen. Schumer contended in a press release that, "We desperately need to improve the background check system, which helps prevent the adjudicated mentally ill and violent criminals from getting their hands on a dangerous weapon."

But mental health professionals were *not exactly on the same page as the perennially anti-gun senator.*

As noted by *Reason*, Prof. James Jacobs, director of the Center for Research in Crime and Justice at the New York University School of Law stated, "There's a lot of criticism about denying more people their Second Amendment rights based on mental illness. Mental health professionals think it will deter people from seeking help and will stigmatize the mentally ill."

That's been a long-standing concern among veterans' advocates, too. Some veterans have complained that their Second Amendment rights – which they served and sometimes fought to protect – have been jeopardized by seeking help with Post Traumatic Stress Disorder, or other impairments.

Here's what the Reason article, authored by J.D. Tuccille, had to say: "(University of Toronto Sociology Prof. Jennifer) Carlson suggests that 'if executed properly, the Schumer bill could address some of these issues.' But if executed poorly—and the federal government does seem to have a bit of a track record for screwing the pooch—Schumer's proposals could make things worse. 'Because these compliance mechanisms fall under administrative procedure,' says Carlson, 'there is no expectation of due process.' That threatens to turn what the funny Schumer describes as 'sensible measures and restrictions' into nothing more than collections of increasingly sensitive data with which to be arbitrary."

Being arbitrary about gun laws has been something of a habit with the federal government, and Schumer has supported legislation that resulted in this situation.

In summing up the Schumer effort, Tuccille had this to say: "If history is any guide, the Schumers and their friends will keep coming back with schemes to subject us to the arbitrary dictates of an already bloated criminal justice system. These schemes will, again, stand little hope of preventing the crimes at which they're allegedly targeted—or of being obeyed by the people subject to their dictates."

And then there's stupidity

Demagoguery is one fault of government when it comes to firearms. Blatant stupidity is another, and this may be best exemplified by something that happened in the miserably anti-gun state of Hawaii when the Honolulu Police Department decided to replace its inventory of Smith & Wesson duty sidearms with semiautomatic pistols from Glock during the summer of 2015. What transpired, as detailed by Fox News at the time, was such a horrendous example of political correctness overkill that it is difficult to judge by comparison to any other incident.

Instead of trading in some 2,300 pistols including about 200 that were new in the box and had apparently never been issued or used (departments keep spare firearms on hand in case of a mechanical failure or if one becomes a piece of evidence in a shooting inves-

tigation) – a common practice to help a police department defray costs of re-arming – Honolulu officials
decided instead to have the guns, with an estimated
value of $575,000, melted down.

The result was that more than a half-million dollars'
worth of surplus firearms were denied to law-abiding
citizens and on-duty or retired law enforcement, either
in Hawaii or more likely on the mainland, and that was
a direct slap at the right to carry, not to mention the
taxpayers of Honolulu.

Mayor Kirk Caldwell and police department officials
decided that they did not want the surplus firearms to
be "sold to the general public and end up on the streets
of Honolulu." They even insisted that no parts of the
firearms be allowed to get into public circulation, Fox
News reported.

But the cable news agency, quoting *Hawaii News Now*,
noted, "Selling the guns, with mandatory background
checks to ensure they were only purchased by legal
owners, could have netted the city $575,000."

Before anyone really knew what was happening, the
guns were already destroyed. Co-author Alan Gottlieb,
speaking at the time on behalf of the Second Amendment Foundation, told Fox News that the destruction
of those handguns was "the height of anti-gun stupidity and will not stop one criminal from getting a
weapon."

Facts like that never so much as distract anti-gunners
from their goal of ridding their Utopian dream world
of firearms. Yet the Aloha State has one of the lowest
gun death rates in the nation, Fox News noted, so one
wonders where the problem is. The only "problem" is
in the minds of those whose practice of political cor-

rectness in this case had a half-million-dollar price tag. As the saying goes, that takes a special kind of stupid.

When *Hawaii News Now* initially broke the story, before the meltdown had occurred, it referred to several unidentified police officers who maintained that the pistols still had value, and could be sold, donated or reused. At the time they estimated that even selling the guns for parts would have possibly netted as much as $230,000. That's still a great deal of money that could have been used to offset some department costs.

In the midst of this government waste, one voice of reason surfaced in the Hawaii News Now report. That came from Honolulu City Council Budget Chair Ann Kobayashi.

"I don't understand the thinking of the administration as to getting rid of these guns when we could benefit from the recycling, as long as there are safeguards," she was quoted as observing.

Punish the right people

There is a better approach than anti-gun demagoguery when it comes to reducing violent crime involving firearms. Put the perpetrators in jail for extended stays.

That seemed to be the strategy behind legislation proposed in Wisconsin that would set a mandatory minimum sentence of at least three years for someone with a violent felony record in possession of a gun, and anywhere from 18 months to five years if a person with a record of violent crime commits another crime with a firearm.

When it was reported by WUWM (the local NPR affiliate) in Milwaukee, the story noted that even anti-gun Mayor Tom Barrett supported the idea. Not surprisingly, there was opposition to the idea, with claims that mandatory minimum sentences had not been effective, and that they "promoted disparities" in the system, perhaps meaning that they resulted in people getting locked up who deserved it.

But that argument could just as well be made about the effectiveness of gun control laws, and how they perpetuate disparities when they penalize law-abiding gun owners without hampering the activities of armed criminals.

Perhaps Milwaukee Police Chief Edward Flynn, who has been unfriendly to armed citizens in the past, especially those who open carry, blunted the opposition by explaining that "States that have stronger laws on guns and criminals and putting them in jail have much lower levels of violence than those that don't."

The flip side of this common sense reality came from U.S. Senator Tim Kaine, a Virginia Democrat who seemed to jump on the exploitation bandwagon when, just two weeks after a young news team from Roanoke's WDBJ was murdered on live television during an interview, he introduced the so-called "Responsible Transfer of Firearms Act." All this measure really would do is discourage, if not entirely eliminate (and criminalize) private firearms transactions by requiring retailers and private citizens to take unspecified "reasonable steps" to assure they were not selling firearms to disqualified persons.

Kaine's measure overlooked the fact that private citizens cannot legally access the National Instant Check System. Even if they could, there is no way short of true clairvoyance for anyone to predict what someone might do with a firearm next month that he or she bought *last* month.

The gunman in the WDBJ case was a disgruntled former employee of that station, fired more than a year earlier, but who purchased his firearm from a Virginia gun shop, passing a background check in the process. That Kaine, according to the story in *The Hill*, blamed "loose gun laws for allowing firearms dealers to sell guns to people who are prohibited from owning them" was at best disingenuous.

But that, as this chapter has demonstrated, seems to be part of a pattern among gun control proponents. Pushing legislation that would not have prevented the crime it ostensibly addresses is something of a habit on Capitol Hill and in legislatures all over the country.

They don't even slow down when research reveals just how phony some of their arguments prove to be. Take, for example, a University of Chicago Crime Lab survey, reported by the *Chicago Sun-Times*, of inmates at the Cook County Jail. This survey determined that few gun-toting criminals got their firearms at gun shows or from the Internet, nor do they steal firearms or buy them from a licensed retailer.

This survey essentially supported earlier research about the origin of firearms used in crime that was the subject of a survey for the Department of Justice's Bureau of Justice Statistics. That study, which involved inmate interviews in federal prisons, revealed how criminals get the majority of their firearms from acquaintances, family members or street sources. Rarely (0.07 percent) got their guns at gun shows. One percent got firearms at flea markets, and only 8.3 percent bought them at retail outlets. Another 3.8 percent bought guns at pawn shops.

About 70 percent of the jail inmates interviewed for the Chicago study said they "got their guns from family, fellow gang members or through other social connections. Only two said they bought a gun at a store," the *Sun-Times* reported.

One other thing the Cook County survey revealed that also poked holes in a long-standing contention by the gun prohibition lobby had to do with so-called "assault rifles." The newspaper noted that "Only a handful said they had possessed military-style assault weapons such as an AK-47." But was this widely reported? Naturally not, because it did not fit the gun control narrative.

To suppress such information is dishonest, and for elected officials to ignore it in their efforts to pass increasingly restrict gun control measures is a critical component of their demagoguery. It feeds the delusional impressions among anti-gunners that one type of firearm is bad, and that criminals get their guns by exploiting some non-existent "loophole" at gun shows, which have been unfairly dubbed "arms bazaars for criminals and terrorists."

The 'Proper cause' excuse

Discretionary carry permit laws like the ones in New York, New Jersey and Maryland have allowed some awfully questionable denials, including the one that affected a retired New York Department of Correctional Services and Community Supervision employee named Paul Monpetit. His was hardly a rare example.

According to WWNY News, Monpetit spent more than 20 years working for the agency, and after retiring, he sought to have his carry concealed firearms permit classified as "unrestricted" for potential on-the-street protection against former prison inmates who may have thought they had a score to settle. Unfortunately, this sort of thing has happened over the years in jurisdictions across the country.

But when Monpetit applied for the expanded permit to County Judge Jerome Richards, the application was denied. At the time, WWNY, a Fox News affiliate, reported that the judge had been rejecting quite a few permit applications. Apparently, this was because of a new regulation adopted by the county government that applicants for "unrestricted" concealed carry permits show "proper cause." That was the same requirement that resulted in lawsuits elsewhere, including the District of Columbia, with mixed results in the courts.

According to WWNY, Judge Richards was apparently acting on his interpretation of state penal law dating back to 1980 in a case that was filed against the New York Police Department. This "proper cause" requirement forces a permit applicant to "demonstrate a special need for self-protection." While gun rights activists argue that this sort of thing wouldn't pass the smell test in a shall-issue state, federal courts have ruled in favor of such arbitrary laws, and at this writing, the U.S. Supreme Court had decline review of cases from New York, New Jersey and Maryland, allowing these laws to stand, at least for the time being.

A spokesman for a New York organization called the Northern New York Freedom Fighters summed up the gun owner sentiment when he observed, "If a person is trustworthy with a pistol permit, a firearm permit, to hunt and target shoot, he ought to be trustworthy all the way."

Even in states with shall-issue statutes – where local officials are not allowed to exercise broad and arbitrary discretion – there are other ways of making life tougher for the legally-armed citizen. Look at what happened in Tennessee, for example, when legally-armed citizens found that they could be fired from their jobs for having firearms in their cars, parked and locked on company property.

In Tennessee, which is a state where hunting is hugely popular and at the time this book was written about a half-million citizens had carry permits, it took legislation over the course of two years to provide protections from prosecution and firing. But the fix wasn't a slam dunk.

As Fox News reported at the time, "The amended bill had overwhelming support in Nashville's GOP-dominated Statehouse, but was opposed by a coalition of groups that included Democrats, gun control advocates and the state Chamber of Commerce."

There is considerable debate about such legislation because it amounts to a collision between Second Amendment rights and the private property rights of the property owners. It is a situation that requires a different perspective, because this is not a case of a restaurant or some other establishment declaring itself a "gun free zone" to disarm customers, it's a case of a business owner establishing some guidelines for employees.

One might even find some sympathy for the opponents in the statement from House Democratic Caucus Chair Mike Stewart. Quoted by Fox News.com, he called the legislation "outrageous."

What's next," he wondered. "Are we going to have a law that forces a family to let an armed person into their living room? Where does it stop?"

On the other hand, it is not as if workers were demanding to carry guns on the job, only to have them in their locked vehicles for the trip to and from work, or during the hunting season, from work to the hunting camp. There may be no correct answer to this problem, but the Tennessee Legislature passed a law to protect legally-armed citizens from dismissal if they have a gun in the car, and those lawmakers have lots of company across the states.

As Fox News noted in its report, Tennessee joined some 20 other states where similar laws have been adopted, almost invariably to the chagrin of chambers of commerce and the gun prohibition lobby. For advocates of concealed and open carry, this amounts to a "good start," but it remains unpopular with employers who, regardless of their personal attitudes about firearms, don't like government interfering with their rights as business and property owners.

One must take into consideration the concern of employers about the possibility for a disgruntled or fired worker to go to his or her car and bring back a firearm into the business. The counter to that argument has been that allowing guns in cars gives other employees a "fighting chance" to retrieve their own guns in self-defense.

Indeed, in discussing demagoguery, one might make a legitimate argument that for a legislature to force employers to allow employees to have firearms in their locked cars on company property might also be considered as such. As noted above, there is no easy solution to this dilemma, nor does there appear to be any "middle ground."

You're on one side or the other, and ultimately one side is going to be unhappy.

10: A MATTER OF (DIS)TRUST

"The gun law's intention is to be as difficult and cumbersome as possible."—Alexander Roubian, president of the New Jersey Second Amendment Society, to FoxNews.com.

When Wisconsin Governor Scott Walker announced his support of legislation to end a 48-hour waiting period for the purchase of a handgun in the Badger State, it was the sort of thing that people in the Second Amendment community hail because it makes sense.

No law-abiding citizen, especially one whose life might be in jeopardy, should have to wait for two days before being able to buy a handgun, which even the U.S. Supreme Court in *District of Columbia v. Dick Anthony Heller* in June 2008 noted is the most commonly-used firearm for self-defense. Yet Walker had critics, including columnist James E. Causey, writing for the *Milwaukee Journal Sentinel.* He intimated that Walker was pushing the measure in order to get a favorable rating from the National Rifle Association, when he spoke at their then-upcoming annual convention.

"I've seen firsthand how arguments can quickly escalate to violence, and I certainly don't want to make it that much easier for people to get their hands on handguns — and I say this as a legal gun owner," Causey wrote.

But what would Causey, or those who share his reluctance – call it a distrust – do to address the problem with waiting periods to the friends and family of New Jersey resident Carol Bowne? She had applied for a permit merely to buy a gun to keep at home for personal protection from an ex-boyfriend, a process that is supposed to take 30 days in the Garden State, but is routinely stretched out as long as possible to discourage handgun ownership.

No one could speak with Bowne about this problem because she's dead, stabbed fatally in her own driveway by a man identified as Michael Eitel. Her brutal murder made national headlines for days, because Americans got a chance to see the downside of waiting periods.

Bureaucratic delays and waiting periods for handguns are the government's way of telling citizens that they cannot be trusted with defensive sidearms. It is an alarming and deplorable bit of red tape that, as noted by Alexander Roubian, president of the New Jersey Second Amendment Society, to FoxNews.com when he was asked about the Bowne case, is intended "to be as difficult and cumbersome as possible."

Up in Milwaukee, columnist Causey apparently thinks it is quite acceptable to throw a few roadblocks in the way of a same-day pickup for a defensive handgun. His justification was spelled out by quoting the anti-gun Wisconsin Coalition Against Domestic Violence, which claimed that assaults with firearms "are 12 times more likely to result in death than non-firearm assaults, and an abused woman living in a home with a gun is five times more likely to be killed than an abused woman who does not have a gun in her home."

He also asserted: "Purchasing a gun should not be as easy as buying a big screen television from Wal-Mart. It should require just as much skill and training as a driver's license." Such arguments are over-dramatic, because nobody needs to go through a background check to buy a television, and driving is a privilege, not a constitutionally-protected fundamental civil right recognized in both the Wisconsin and U.S. constitutions.

To his credit, Causey also quoted Nik Clark, president of Wisconsin Carry, Inc., who recalled a series of rapes in the central city.

"When those rapes were taking place and the cops could not catch the rapists why would we tell a woman walking from the bus stop at night to get home that she has to wait to get a gun to protect herself?" Clark wondered.

Indeed. In Carol Bowne's case several states away, it wasn't rape that was feared. It was death, and it came calling just 48 hours after Bowne had gone to her local police department in Berlin Township to find out why there was a delay in the issuance of her gun permit, what Fox News called a "languishing application."

Noted Roubian in the Fox story, "In most states, you go to the store, get a background check, and purchase a weapon. A police chief should have no part of the process. This woman had a legitimate issue and no one helped her."

But in New Jersey, even if Bowne had been able to legally purchase a handgun, it might not have helped her because she was murdered outside of her house. In the Garden State, it is difficult if not impossible for average citizens to get a permit to carry. It is a despicable situation, which has been challenged unsuccessfully in court, with the U.S. Supreme Court cowardly refraining to review a case. Some in the Second Amendment community believe the high court is reluctant to take such a case because they do not want to acknowledge that the "right to bear arms" means the right to carry a gun outside of one's home or business for the purpose of personal defense. Critics say that any Supreme Court justice who holds that opinion should not serve on any court, much less the highest court in the land.

Bowne's killer was found two days after her murder, in the garage of another ex-girlfriend, dead. He had hanged himself, though it was erroneously reported at one point that he had died from a self-inflicted gunshot wound. It was an appropriately self-administered death penalty for his heinous crime, which was captured on the security camera at Bowne's residence. But it did not bring back his innocent victim.

Pushing laws that don't work

When former Maryland Governor Martin O'Malley put forth his gun control manifesto during the early days of the Democrat race for the party's 2016 presidential nomination, a large section was devoted to protecting women from so-called "gun violence." (There's that term again, as though someone stabbed or bludgeoned to death was somehow less victimized than a person who had been fatally shot.)

But O'Malley's scheme was not really about protecting women. It was about adding layers of red tape to the lawful purchase and ownership of firearms, including the establishment of a national gun registry, the licensing and fingerprinting of gun owners, the mandating of a waiting period on firearms transactions and a requirement of "safe storage," however that was defined.

The entire plan suggested a visceral distrust of gun owners, and it raised red flags throughout the gun community immediately. The Citizens Committee for the Right to Keep and Bear Arms (CCRKBA) called it a "disturbing document for any number of reasons." Second Amendment activists called it much worse on social media, and many said it was the signal that O'Malley's presidential bid was going to end on a sour note.

Perhaps most disturbing, however, is the fact that far too many people on the political left agreed with O'Malley's scheme, while lacking the backbone and intestinal fortitude to actually admit it. The document read like a gun prohibition wish list; all the things that strike raw nerves within the gun rights movement.

Calling these suggestions "commonsense measures," the O'Malley team intimated that they would "dramatically reduce gun-related homicides, suicides and trafficking." What it really demonstrated was that the ex-governor, a devoted anti-gunner, was essentially clueless when it came to the criminal trafficking and acquisition of firearms.

Criminals don't bother with background checks, yet O'Malley insisted that they would be part of his program if he became president.

Criminals don't bother with waiting periods, while O'Malley (and the people supporting his extremist agenda) believes they will prevent crimes and suicides. Or, at least, that is what he says publicly. Many suspect that this is really just a scheme to discourage law-abiding citizens from exercising their rights, because – in the minds of extremist anti-gunners – average citizens cannot be trusted with firearms.

Probably to the shock of CNN, the cable network that carried the second Republican presidential debate-turned-donnybrook (by design) in September

2015, Florida Sen. Marco Rubio put it in the proper perspective in less than 30 seconds when, well into the second hour, he addressed a question on gun rights.

"First of all," Rubio stated matter-of-factly, "the only people that follow the law are law abiding people. Criminals, by definition, ignore the law, so you can pass all the gun laws in the world — like the left wants — (and) criminals are going to ignore it because they are criminals."

Of course, that level-headed logic never seems to get through to Rubio's anti-gun Senate colleagues, including Virginia Democrat Tim Kaine. Following the on-air shooting of two reporters from Roanoke's WDBJ, Kaine introduced the *"Responsible Transfer of Firearms Act."* It was a questionable piece of legislation that would change federal gun law to require gun sellers to take "reasonable steps" – without defining specifically what such steps might entail – to assure that the buyer can legally own a firearm.

Almost immediately, CCRKBA reacted to the proposal, accusing Kaine of writing legislation that was "intentionally vague and designed to create a chilling effect, especially on perfectly legal private firearms transactions."

"It appears Sen. Kaine also expects gun dealers and private sellers to be clairvoyant," the organization said in a press release. "Just what else could a retailer do beyond a background check? Sen. Kaine seems to suggest background checks on all transactions may not be good enough. The bill just talks about 'reasonable steps,' but what does that mean, especially to a private seller?"

Kaine's legislation would not have prevented the WDBJ gunman from obtaining a firearm because he did not have a criminal background, nor had he ever been adjudicated mentally deficient. He had been fired from the station more than a year before the shooting.

But it is this sort of legislation that anti-gunners consistently introduce, suggesting that they want to place as many discouraging roadblocks as possible in the way of legal gun ownership, and that seems to reflect an underlying distrust of people who either own guns or want to.

If laws can be written to discourage gun ownership, anti-gunners figure that fewer people will be inclined to exercise their right to carry defensive firearms, and ultimately, own guns altogether.

When you know a law doesn't work

The most widespread manifestation of distrust toward gun owners by the gun prohibition lobby and their anti-gun legislative colleagues is the background check.

In the early 1990s during the first Clinton administration, passage of the Brady Handgun Act included the creation of the National Instant Check System, designed to make such background checks palatable by building a database of convicted criminals and those who had been confined to mental institutions and/or adjudicated mentally incompetent.

Nowadays, in order to buy a gun at retail, one must pass a background check. In order to qualify for a concealed carry license or permit, one must also pass a background check. Therefore, would it not seem acceptable to gun control proponents that a citizen with a current, valid carry license be exempted from background checks for gun sales while his permit/license is active? That's not good enough for the anti-gun lobby.

In a survey of 2,002 adults in the summer of 2015, the Pew Research Center found continued strong public support for background checks on all firearms purchases, including private transactions and sales at gun shows. The affirmative figure hovered at 85 percent, with Democrats at 88 percent and Republicans at 79 percent.

Pew reported equally strong support for laws aimed at preventing mentally ill people from purchasing guns, although once again, the "devil is in the details" of such legislation, because such legislative proposals invariably inconvenience more honest citizens than ever manage to snare a mentally ill person who carries a gun.

But, as writer Alex Yablon at *The Trace* noted in an essay about the paradox that exists among people who support background checks, but also doubt that they actually prevent the wrong people from getting their hands on guns.

"(T)hough many say that gun violence is an increasingly important issue, a majority don't think that the most commonly debated policy fix would make a difference," Yablon observed.

That "policy fix" is the background check. Many in the gun rights movement are convinced that the so-called "universal background check" push by Michael Bloomberg's Everytown for Gun Safety and its various state level affiliates to make such checks the law of the land is really aimed at eventually establishing a gun registry.

Yablon was writing about a CNN/ORC International poll on guns that occurred in late summer 2015. That poll, he said, "which showed tepid belief that a stronger background check system would effectively keep guns out of the hands of people with serious criminal records or severe mental illness." This begs the question, "If you don't think something is really going to work, why support it?"

The most common reply to that query runs along this philosophy: "Well, we have to do *something*. I just feel that we need to make an effort."

The impression one comes away with from such a conversation is that the appearance of having done something to reduce the bloodshed is enough to make one feel good about their actions. It's illusory, of course, but this is more about "feelings" than fact.

Yablon portrayed something of the same conclusion in his article when he quoted Kevin Ingham of Strategies 360, which he described as a "Democratic-leaning policy polling and focus group."

The article noted, "Just because some laws don't always stop the behavior they target, Ingham says, doesn't mean people think they aren't worthwhile: 'It's common sense that we should at least be *trying* to make it harder for people who want to do bad things to get guns'."

This is a reflection of what Alexander Roubian from the New Jersey Second Amendment Society, quoted at the beginning of this chapter, had to say.

In California, Oregon and Washington, *all* transfers of firearms including private sales or gifts require a background check, with few exceptions. Still, that hasn't prevented violent street gangs or mentally dangerous people from obtaining firearms. Elliot Rodger, the Santa Barbara spree killer passed three background checks to purchase three different handguns. He also went through three 10-day state-mandated waiting periods for those firearms. He did not have a carry permit. He stabbed three of his victims and shot three others. And today, he is typically remembered as the "Santa Barbara *gunman*."

But there's an interesting postscript. In 2014, a federal judge in California struck down that state's 10-day waiting period requirement for current gun owners who have already passed a background check. The ruling also exempted people who have a permit to own a gun. It was a smack in the face to restrictive gun law advocates, but hardly a total victory for Second Amendment activists. Essentially, the ruling by Judge Anthony W. Ishii made common sense out of something less, by explaining in so many words that requiring somebody who has recently undergone a waiting period to buy a gun when that person already owns a gun is rather superfluous. If the individual was intending to do harm, he/she wouldn't bother buying a new firearm, they would simply use one they already own.

Smearing the law-abiding

Another effort by anti-gunners to discourage carrying firearms is the demonization of people who do. Most notable of these campaigns is the one promoted by the anti-gun Violence Policy Center (VPC) called "Concealed Carry Killers." This effort to stigmatize legally-armed citizens may have varying degrees of success or failure, depending upon the part of the country one happens to be standing in.

This VPC website is rather self-explanatory in its mission: "Concealed carry killers are a threat to public safety. The evidence is clear that all too often, private citizens use their concealed handguns to take lives, not to save them."

A popular blog site, *The Truth About Guns*, called the VPC's running report "a piece which twists facts to scare people into believing that armed citizens are really just bloodthirsty savages bent on murder and mayhem."

The VPC makes no effort to separate homicides from suicides and contends that "Only a tiny fraction of these cases are ever ruled to be in self-defense. Any homicide that is legally determined to be in self-defense is documented and removed from the *Concealed Carry Killers* database and the ongoing tallies."

Regardless, the seed is planted in the minds of many people who don't bother to do a little math, that citizens with carry permits/licenses are untrustworthy loons. Those who actually do some math can come up with a better idea of what goes on.

As noted earlier in this book, the most current estimate of the number of legally-licensed private citizens across the United States is more than 12 *million*. According to the VPC's website, at the time of this writing, there had allegedly been 750 incidents of people being killed or committing suicide who had carry licenses. That comes to such a miniscule fraction of one percent that it wouldn't even register on a scale.

But the VPC would have millions of law-abiding citizens who had harmed nobody judged by the actions of a few. That would be tantamount to criminalizing all African Americans because a tiny percentage of the overall black population have committed crimes, or classifying all Muslims as terrorists because of the actions of some fanatics.

The VPC and other gun control groups never, *ever* acknowledge the hypocrisy of their leaders. The Truth About Guns article mentioned a few paragraphs ago was about Shannon Watts, founder of the anti-gun Moms Demand Action for Gun Sense in America. In that piece, Watts was criticized for having bodyguards when she makes public appearances.

Other well-known anti-gunners, most notably billionaire Michael Bloomberg and New York Gov. Andrew Cuomo, have armed security. This bit of hypocrisy prompted somebody to do a bit of artwork that has become popular on social media that says "People With Armed Security Should Probably Shut Up About Gun Control."

But, of course, they don't.

Waiting periods

The anti-gun Law Center to Prevent Gun Violence (LCPGV) has been big in promoting waiting periods that, according to their own website, require "a specified number of days elapse between the time a firearm is purchased and it is physically transferred to the purchaser." This approach also presumes that every gun buyer is just waiting to create havoc.

This website adds, "The goals of a waiting period are to: (1) give law enforcement officials sufficient time to perform a background check; and (2) provide a 'cooling off' period to help guard against impulsive acts of violence."

How long a waiting period would this group support? Perhaps the answer can be found in their "Waiting Periods Policy Summary."

"The average time it takes for the FBI to determine that illegal purchasers are ineligible to receive firearms is 25 days," their statement explains. "As a result, *the FBI has recommended extending the research time to complete background checks* (emphasis in original) to reduce the number of prohibited people who are able to purchase firearms by default."

A waiting period of nearly a month is not for "cooling off," it's to discourage the exercise of a civil right.

The LCPGV has gone so far as to offer some "model laws" aimed at creating "a safer America." Among these one can find suggestions dealing with open and concealed carry. Here's a short version: 1) require background checks on all gun purchasers; 2) license firearm owners; 3) register all firearms; 4) regulate firearms dealers and ammunition sellers; 5) require the reporting of lost or stolen firearms; 6) impose a waiting period before the sale of a firearm; and 7) limit firearm purchases to one per person every 90 days.

That last one underscores what the NRA, CCRKBA and other Second Amendment groups have said about so-called "one-gun-a-month" laws. Once the government gets away with limiting someone to a single gun purchase per month, the government can expand that limitation, in this case one every three months. But if that is adopted, what would prevent a new limit of one gun in a calendar year? Carried through to a logical conclusion, the limit would then become one firearm in a lifetime and then no firearms at all.

The right to keep and bear arms would become a historical footnote. If there is still anyone who questions or dismisses the "slippery slope" argument, this document should put that doubt to rest. To suggest otherwise is to live in complete denial.

Agenda-driven 'research'

There are various studies that all seem designed to tell the downside of gun ownership, and in Autumn 2015, researchers at Boston University and Harvard University claimed that teens are less likely to illegally carry guns in states with tougher gun control laws. The study got widespread attention from Reuters and other agencies including U.S. News, and the study results were none too kind to the right to keep and bear arms.

Reuters quoted Dr. Eric Fleeger, described as an emergency medicine specialist at Boston Children's Hospital.

"If parents own a gun, the safest approach is to store them outside of the home such as in a bank vault," Fleeger advised. "If they are stored at home it is essential to store them safety locked, separated from locked ammunition."

Right, in the event of a home invasion robbery or some natural or man-made disaster, what is the gun owner supposed to do, ask the criminals to wait until morning when the homeowner can dash to the bank, retrieve his or her gun, and return home to fight back?

Reuters described the researchers' efforts as an analysis of data on teenage gun possession pulled from a survey of high school students in 38 states. The study compared firearms regulations in each of the states, including whether so-called "assault weapons" were banned, and whether there were "limitations on use in public places."

Another story in *U.S. News* quoted one of the researchers, Ziming Xuan, who stated, "It's very likely explained by the fact that the youth are getting their guns from adults. If a state with strong gun control is able to reduce the amount of adult gun ownership, it will reduce the number of kids carrying guns."

That story also quoted Sam Bieler, research associate at the Urban Institute in Washington, D.C., who had this observation. "The tendency of youth to carry firearms is related to the legal environment they're growing up in. This is something that states should be keeping in mind as they consider their gun control laws."

That makes sense, right? Translation: "If we seriously restrict the rights of law-abiding citizens, we'll see fewer guns used by teenage thugs."

That's essentially what one other person who spoke with *U.S. News* had to say. From that publication's own story: "This relationship appears to hinge on adult gun ownership, the researchers found. If restrictive gun laws lower the rate of adult gun ownership, then teens are less likely to have guns to carry around, according to their findings.

"Bindu Kalesan, an adjunct assistant professor at Columbia University's Mailman School of Public Health in New York City, said that this study is 'basically saying, adult gun ownership is the real problem.' She was not involved with the research," *U.S. News* noted.

Untrustworthy government

Trust and distrust are double-edged swords. Where politicians and prohibitionists have displayed what approaches a seething distrust of American gun owners, the flip side of this has been amply revealed by polls conducted by Gallup and Rasmussen which show that American citizens do not trust government, and perhaps justifiably so.

When has government ever given up authority over the governed?

When has a bureaucracy ever been completely dismantled, employees dismissed and funding ended?

In late September 2015, Gallup published the results of a poll that revealed nearly half of Americans (49 percent) believe the federal government – you know, the *United States government* – poses "an immediate threat to the rights and freedoms of ordinary citizens." It was a startling revelation, but according to Gallup, very much in line with similar surveys over the previous five years.

According to Gallup at the time, "The lower percentage of Americans agreeing in 2003 that the federal government posed an immediate threat likely reflected the more positive attitudes about government evident after the 9/11 terrorist attacks. The percentage gradually increased to 44% by 2006, and then reached the 46% to 49% range in four surveys conducted since 2010."

Because the poll dated back to only 2010, this was one that the Obama administration had to own. The blame-someone-else president could not lay this government distrust at the feet of his predecessor, George W. Bush.

But Gallup did note that there was at least a bit of political partisanship in the responses of those participating in the poll. Here's how Gallup explained it:

"The remarkable finding about these attitudes is how much they reflect apparent antipathy toward the party controlling the White House, rather than being a purely fundamental or fixed philosophical attitude about government.

"Across the four surveys conducted during the Republican administration of George W. Bush, Democrats and Democratic-leaning independents were consistently more likely than Republicans and Republican-leaning independents to say the federal government posed an immediate threat.

"By contrast, across the four most recent surveys conducted during the Democratic Obama administration, the partisan gap flipped, with Republicans significantly more likely to agree.

"Republican agreement with the "immediate threat" statement has been higher during the Obama administration than was Democratic agreement during the Bush administration, thus accounting for the overall rise in agreement across all national adults."

And there was something else buried in the report from Gallup: "The most frequently mentioned specific threats involve gun control laws and violations of the Second Amendment to the Constitution, mentioned by 12% who perceive the government to be an immediate threat."

But in its report, Gallup tried to play down the situation as a matter more about dislike of the president than widespread angst over government.

"The fact that almost half of Americans see the federal government as an immediate threat to their lives and freedoms may appear alarming at first, perhaps conjuring an image of Americans worrying that the government will be breaking down their doors and engaging in random arrests of private citizens.

"But two findings mitigate against this type of more dramatic interpretation. First, the fact that Democrats and Republicans have flipped in their probability of holding these views when the administration changed in 2009 shows that these attitudes reflect more of a response to the president and disagreement with his policies than a fundamental feeling about the federal government in general.

"Second, the explanations offered by those who hold this view reveal more traditional or political types of complaints about things the government is doing, rather than more radical beliefs about the government using power or force against its citizens."

The Gallup survey was based on telephone interviews with a random sample of 1,025 adults aged 18 and over across the United States and the District of Columbia.

Gallup is not the only game in town when it comes to polling. Rasmussen ran a couple of surveys that strongly suggest there is widespread distrust of the government among the citizens, especially when it comes to gun rights.

Within 24 hours of the Gallup poll revelation, Rasmussen Reports announced that most voters in its poll do not believe the federal government should be the final authority on who owns firearms, and they also didn't warm up to the notion of a country where only police and military personnel have guns.

That survey, taken from among 1,000 likely voters with a plus/minus sampling error of three percentage points, found only 34 percent support for the idea that responsibility for gun laws dealing with ownership should be placed in the hands of the federal government. Thirty-six percent think it should be handled by the state, and 18 percent believed that local government should be the final arbiter.

Reaction from gun rights activists was predictable. Many felt that the Constitution and Bill of Rights provide the "final word" on gun ownership.

More than a year earlier, Rasmussen had asked people about gun control and learned that most people (71 percent) believe it to be an impossible task to completely prevent mass shootings. That survey was taken in the wake of the attack on the Navy Yard in Washington, D.C.

The more stunning revelation from this survey was that 62 percent of the people do not trust the government to fairly administer gun control laws. Only 26 percent of those surveyed at the time did trust the government to fairly enforce those laws, and 12 percent were not sure.

How has government become the target of such public distrust, especially when it comes to Second Amendment rights?

To paraphrase an old commercial about banking and investment: "The old-fashioned way. Government earned it."

The Kates-Mauser study

Some time ago, a study that was published in the *Harvard Journal of Law & Public Policy* indicated that "the more guns a nation has, the less criminal activity," according to a story about the study that appeared on BeliefNet.com.

Now, what's this all about, and why does it have to do with distrust? First and foremost, this study was largely, and perhaps deliberately, ignored, the BriefNet.com report suggested. Authored by Don B. Kates, a Yale graduate, criminologist and constitutional lawyer, and

Gary Mauser, a graduate of the University of California, Irvine and a Canadian criminologist, the findings simply don't match the anti-gun narrative. It was titled *Would banning firearms reduce murder and suicide?*

When BeliefNet.com Senior Editor Rob Kerby wrote a lengthy report about the study, it spread across social media.

The Kates-Mauser paper first got the attention of Michael Snyder, writing at the "End of the American Dream" blog in August 2013. In his piece, headlined "18 Little-Known Gun Facts That Prove That Guns Make Us Safer," Snyder offered tiny points from the study. Kerby's lengthier article went into greater depth, leading the reader straight back to the original document, and it is worth reading.

Among the revelations from Kates and Mauser that undoubtedly made their report toxic among the gun prohibitionist was this tidbit: "In the late 1990s, England moved from stringent controls to a complete ban of all handguns and many types of long guns. Hundreds of thousands of guns were confiscated from those owners law-abiding enough to turn them in to authorities. Without suggesting this caused violence, the ban's ineffectiveness was such that by the year 2000 violent crime had so increased that England and Wales had Europe's highest violent crime rate, far surpassing even the United States."

Gun control proponents have long pointed to the way England regulates firearms ownership as a model of propriety that should be followed in the United States. By sharing information that tends to poke holes in that effort, it might put the campaign to thwart Second Amendment activism off the rails.

It should be noted that Great Britain has also experienced something of a phenomenon in the rise of knife-related crime. It has become so worrisome that there has been a campaign to "save lives" by doing away with knives. What would medieval knights, who carried broadswords, think of such an effort? Probably not much. But we digress.

Hmmm? If you can't trust the media to make as big a deal of the Kates-Mauser paper as it might the findings of some anti-gun study, it only reinforces the notion that the mainstream media is biased against guns, gun owners and research that contends firearms are not so bad, after all.

Why sweep such information to the corner, if that is, indeed, what actually happened? One possible explanation is that this kind of research would reinforce the push toward right-to-carry laws and the exercise of Second Amendment rights to keep and bear arms. Understand this: Anything that remotely supports the right to own guns, much less the right to carry defensive sidearms, is likely to be either ignored, demonized or both in an effort to minimize its value in the public discourse regarding firearms.

And this may bring us to the proverbial "bottom line." Extremist anti-gunners simply do not trust their fellow humans with firearms. They only equate bad firearms use with all firearms use. Many are anti-hunters who would very much like to disarm the nation's millions of sportsmen and women in order to save Bambi. Others have wrongly concluded that all gun owners are of the same ilk as the savages that have turned some inner cities into shooting galleries, typically with guns that were illegally obtained and illegally carried. And another subset simply hates guns because they are afraid of the power of firearms, and somehow uncomfortable with the independence and self-reliance that gun possession exemplifies.

People who have guns do not have to huddle with the masses in emergencies, waiting for a benevolent government to come around and take care of them. People with guns can fight back, rather than wait to be rescued by government-authorized saviors who almost invariably arrive too late to effect such a rescue. Fighting back is violent and dangerous. It is risky.

It is also preferable to being butchered.

And finally, there is the widespread philosophy among many activist firearms owners that people with guns can resist. One thing that seems consistent among gun prohibitionists is the belief that they know better how everyone should live than the people upon whom they are attempting to mandate their views. They do not care to have people tell them 'No.'"

So, keep this in perspective: The United States might never have become a reality without people with guns who were willing to fight an oppressive Crown government and risk the dangers that go along with armed resistance. Texas might never have won independence from Mexico had it not been for people with guns.

In the two world wars, America became the "arsenal of freedom." Somewhere in all of this is a moral for the anti-gun set to ponder. Had it not been for firearms, none of these people would be living in a social environment that allows for such freedom of thought and expression.

No real safety concern

When Maine's "constitutional carry" law took effect on Oct. 15, 2015, two important newspaper stories unintentionally showed what gun owners often face when their rights are expanded beyond the comfort zone of some officials.

The *Portland Press Herald* interviewed that city's police chief, Michael Sauschuck, who contended, "This will make our jobs more difficult. I think this law was misguided. We continue to go the wrong way on gun legislation." By no great coincidence, the law had been opposed by the state Chiefs of Police Association and the Maine Sheriffs Association, but the Maine State Police supported the measure, and so did pro-rights Gov. Paul LePage, who signed the bill intio law.

On the same day, the *Bangor Daily News* published comments from a retired police officer who also preferred the permit system. He argued that permits required background checks, fingerprints, a mental health check and proficiency test. Retired cop Dusty Rhodes reportedly told the newspaper, "My concern is some young fellow will accidentally shoot himself or will grab a gun, instead of a knife, and shoot someone else without really knowing what he is doing. It's just going to cause more problems. I hope I'm wrong. Only time will tell."

Indeed, time will tell, as it has already told in the handful of other states where constitutional carry (discussed in Chapter Five) has become law. Legally-armed private citizens do not constitute a threat to public safety. That much was made clear by a firearms instructor identified as Adam Foster. He told the *Press Herald* that he had previously lived in Alaska, a state where carry without a permit has been around for a while. Going to permitless carry did not cause shock waves.

"The world continued to turn round and round," he told the newspaper. "Nothing changed, really. There were no wild, crazy gunfights in the street."

His sarcasm was an allusion to the old "gunfights-in-the-street" scare rhetoric from gun prohibitionists. That has been the prediction repeatedly put forth by anti-gunners repeatedly as they opposed concealed carry reform laws in the late 20th Century. However, statistics do not and never have supported this specious argument.

During the same week that the Maine constitutional carry law took effect, the National Shooting Sports Foundation reported in its weekly on-line newsletter Bullet Points that, "Historical data from FBI Uniform Crime Reports show significant decreases in both the number of annual violent crimes committed as well as the violent crime rate in the United States.

"The figures show a 35.2 percent decline in violent crimes over the past 20 years and a 16.2 percent decline over the past 10 years," NSSF reported. "The continuing decrease in violent crime comes at a time when firearms ownership have (sic) increased significantly across America, a fact that utterly contradicts the mantra of anti-gun groups that more guns equals more crime."

Whether it's a newspaper columnist or a police official used to having some sway over who gets to carry a defensive sidearm in his or her jurisdiction, Second Amendment activists have to overcome those concerns and refute them with evidence, and no small amount of good behavior with firearms. Face it, there are many in the mainstream press who will never have the same devotion to the Second Amendment as they do the First, and they are constantly on the lookout for incidents that support their apprehensions, such as armed citizens firing at shoplifters, or having accidents with firearms in public.

Likewise, there are some career law enforcement officials who prefer to have that power over average citizens; the authority to approve or deny a carry permit or license, or they simply want a system in place to vet private citizens who want to carry for their own protection. Even in a "shall issue" system, the law generally allows denials for good cause.

In the latter case, one can acknowledge concerns about the inability of patrol officers under someone's command being unable to rapidly figure out whether someone is carrying legally or may be up to some nefarious purpose, and is therefore packing illegally. Since none of us are clairvoyant, it is an impossible task to determine with ironclad certainty what some armed citizen's intentions might be at a given moment.

In the former cases – and no one is suggesting that this was the case with the Portland top cop who has a right to offer an opinion from his perspective – there are police and public officials in other states including New York, New Jersey, Massachusetts and Maryland, who hold an inordinate sway over the individual citizen's right to bear arms.

While one can often overcome the concerns of public officials through education and example, it is an impossible task to overcome the prejudices of diehard gun prohibitionists. Perhaps best explained by syndicated conservative columnist Thomas Sowell in a piece he authored that appeared in several newspapers, including the Vancouver Columbian, anti-gun zealots have their minds made up so don't try to confuse them with the facts.

"But if hard evidence shows that restrictions on gun ownership lead to more gun crimes," Sowell wrote, "rather than less, then the National Rifle Association's opposition to those restrictions makes sense, independently of the Second Amendment.

"Since this all boils down to a question of hard evidence about plain facts," he continued, "it is difficult to understand how gun-control laws should have become such a heated and long-lasting controversy."

Noting that there exists "mountains of data" upon which one side or the other could build its case for or against restrictive gun control laws and their relation to violent crime – and specifically homicides – Sowell posited, "With so many facts available from so many places and times, why is gun control still a heated issue? The short answer is that most gun-control zealots do not even discuss the issue in terms of hard facts.

"The zealots act as if they just know — somehow — that bullets will be flying hither and yon if you allow ordinary people to have guns. Among the many facts this ignores is that gun sales were going up in late 20th century America, and the murder rate was going down at the same time."

In a subsequent column, Sowell continued bashing anti-gunners, observing, "The grand illusion of zealots for laws preventing ordinary, law-abiding people from having guns is that 'gun control' laws actually control guns. In a country with many millions of guns, not all of them registered, this is a fantasy and a farce.

"Guns do not vanish into thin air because there are gun control laws," he stated. "Guns -- whether legal or illegal -- can last for centuries. Passing laws against guns may enable zealots to feel good about themselves, but at the cost of other people's lives."

"Why anyone would think that criminals who disobey other laws, including laws against murder, would obey gun control laws is a mystery," Sowell added. "A disarmed population makes crime a safer occupation and street violence a safer sport."

Sowell was driving a stake at the heart of the gun control movement. What rules the anti-gun crowd – the people who endeavor to prevent the full exercise of the Second Amendment right to keep and bear arms – is raw, and deliberately blind, emotion. Whether that emotion is fear of guns or hatred of them, or a combination of both sprinkled, perhaps, with a large dose of elitism, the outcome is the same. The gun control crowd wants to control guns out of existence, at least among average citizens.

"Are there dangers in a widespread availability of guns," Sowell asked in one column. "Yes! And one innocent death is one too many. But what makes anyone think that there are no innocent lives lost by disarming law-abiding people while criminals remain armed?"

Therein lays possibly a hint about strategy for Second Amendment advocates. Guns, especially those carried by private citizens for personal protection, aren't weapons of destruct but emergency survival tools. People don't carry guns to commit violence, but to protect themselves from violence.

San Bernardino lesson

The understanding that armed citizens just might be a force for good was driven home decisively in the wake of the December 2015 terrorist attack in San Bernardino, which was followed by a spike in concealed carry permit applications in several jurisdictions. Likewise, the tragedy "caused a spike in gun sales," according to a report in *Christian Today*.

Quoting Reuters, the news organ noted that after San Bernardino, "Gun retailers are reporting surging sales, with customers saying they want to keep handguns and rifles at hand for self-defense in the event of another attack." The story also quoted gun dealers who confirmed the uptick in sales, which were further inflamed by talk of additional gun control by President Obama and Democrat Hillary Rodham Clinton.

If anything, those remarks continued to demonstrate possibly how out of touch with the average citizen both Obama and Clinton seemed to be. Only a few days after the San Bernardino attack, a Rasmussen poll revealed that a majority of Americans were comfortable in the presence of armed private citizens. Fifty-seven percent of poll respondents told Rasmussen that they were "unconcerned about their safety around those who have legal permits to carry concealed weapons."

Perhaps most interesting of all about that survey was the revelation that 40 percent of the respondents believed that the presence of armed citizens would decrease the number of people killed in a violent incident, while 31 percent thought the opposite. Men were more likely to believe armed citizens could make a difference, and split along party lines, 59 percent of Republicans and 41 percent of independents, but only 25 percent of Democrats thought armed citizens could help.

Perhaps the best example of public officials demonstrating trust in their constituents came from county sheriffs following the San Bernardino attack. The sheriff of Boone County, Ohio advised citizens via his Facebook page to start packing their guns.

The newspaper quoted Sheriff Michael Helmig stating, "I would also like to remind the people who have applied, been trained, and issued a license to carry a Concealed Deadly Weapon (CCDW) that they also have a responsibility to carry their firearm, which they are proficient with, for the safety of themselves and others. It is also the responsibility of everyone to refresh themselves with the laws that govern the privilege and great responsibility that accompany being a CCDW license holder. What else can you do?"

Likewise, Sheriff Paul J. Van Blarcum of Ulster County, N.Y. posted a message on his Facebook page encouraging his licensed citizens to do the same thing. *CBS News* reported his remarks.

The fact that the San Bernardino shooting occurred in a county building where no guns were allowed, even if there had been someone among the victims who could legally carry, was kept out of the headlines except on social media and among some bloggers. As noted in Chapter Six, this business of forcing citizens to leave their self-defense rights at the door is losing ground except among the most ardent anti-gunners.

Gun prohibition extremists simply despise the fact that so many millions of Americans are legally armed, and nothing will likely sway their attitudes, not even rooms full of people who die because they cannot defend themselves.

11: WE NEED TO SETTLE THIS NOW

"Confrontations are not limited to the home." – U.S.
District Judge Richard Posner, Seventh U.S. Circuit Court of
Appeals, *Moore v. Madigan*

"A citizen may not be required to offer a 'good and substantial reason' why he should be permitted to exercise his rights. The right's existence is all the reason he needs."— U.S. District
Judge Benson Everett Legg, District of Maryland, *Woollard v.
Sheridan*

Following the terrorist attacks in Paris and then San
Bernardino, there was a dramatic shift in public attitudes about firearms ownership and defensive carry
among many people who had until then been somewhat indifferent, or ironically had been apprehensive
about guns and the folks who owned them.

All of a sudden, firearms ownership made sense and
the local gun shop was the place to go. People who
had never owned a gun, and some who had never even
considered it, were lining up literally to purchase whatever kind of firearm they could afford. As *ABC News*
reported from a gun shop in San Bernardino, a line had
formed outside of Turner's Outdoorsman, one of the
most popular chains in the Golden State.

The news crew encountered a man who was there to
purchase his first firearm. He told ABC that the attack

"hit a little close to home. It can happen anywhere, and this just shows it."

Isn't it funny how that works out? Many people remain rather lethargic toward the exercise of the right to keep and bear arms up to the moment they suddenly discover that violence can happen anywhere, it doesn't occur on a pre-arranged schedule and criminals – and now terrorists – *never* call ahead to schedule an appointment.

Rasmussen Reports revealed the results of two telephone surveys that underscored the change in public attitude, which could not have helped the gun prohibition lobby at all. In one report, a majority of American adults were found to be "unconcerned about their safety around those who have legal permits to carry concealed weapons." At a time when anti-gun extremists once might have been able to convince people that concealed carry was the act of a paranoid loon, in the wake of San Bernardino, many Americans no longer saw it that way.

Fifty-seven percent of the survey respondents would not run for cover if they suddenly discovered a law-abiding armed citizen were in their midst. The survey also said that 40 percent of the people "believe the presence of more Americans with concealed carry gun permits will decrease the number of people killed in violent incidents in America."

The second *Rasmussen Report* survey said 61 percent of American adults believe, to one degree or another, that the National Rifle Association supports gun policies that make all Americans safer. Thirty-five percent (more than half) of those *responding in the positive* said they "strongly agree" with that assessment.

At the same time, the Rasmussen survey, taken with the *New York Daily News*, said only 29 percent of the respondents did not believe policies advocated by the NRA made the country safer.

This second poll found out something else. Fifty-one percent of the respondents believed additional gun control laws were "more likely to make it harder for law-abiding citizens to purchase a gun rather than keep guns out of the hands of criminals, people with mental illness and suspected terrorists."

Whatever else the Rasmussen surveys accomplished, they amounted to a slap in the face of gun control advocates, including President Obama, and a rejection of their mantra about gun restrictions making communities safer.

All of this brings us around to something of a mystery. The courts remain divided on the right to carry, with the Supreme Court, at this writing, exhibiting a frustrating reluctance to review a case from the lower federal appeals courts that involves the right to carry outside of one's home, for personal protection, and it is not because they have lacked opportunities to take up a case.

The death of conservative Justice Antonin Scalia created a major tremor in the gun rights community. He authored the landmark Second Amendment ruling in *District of Columbia v. Dick Anthony Heller*, and there were immediate concerns that the loss of his influence on the high court could mean serious trouble for the right to keep and bear arms.

Before Scalia died, some people wondered why the high court was reluctant to take a case? One theory is that the court just is not ready to put the issue to rest once and for all, and that they only really have one possible direction to go, especially in the wake of the *Heller* and *McDonald* rulings in 2008 and 2010, respectively. That would be the affirmation that the right to carry extends outside the home, and that as a fundamental civil right ("to bear arms") it cannot be limited to those who provide a "good reason," which is arbitrarily determined by a public official or police chief who opposes the notion of honest citizens carrying guns on the street and in public in a peaceable manner.

Others suggest that the high court's reluctance – the justices have already, at this writing, rejected four cases, from New York, New Jersey, Connecticut and Maryland that directly challenged the arbitrary nature of so-called "shall issue" statutes – is because there were not enough certain votes to make the individual right affirmation on carry in public. If that's accurate, it is a preposterous position for Supreme Court justices to take, for a civil right that is limited to the confines of one's home and/or place of business would be no civil right at all, but half of a right, or a heavily-regulated privilege. With Scalia's passing, those concerns were amplified.

But headway is being made on that front.

The Second Amendment Foundation (SAF) successfully challenged a carry prohibition in Washington, D.C. in a case known as *Palmer v. District of Columbia.* U.S. District Court Judge Frederick J. Scullin declared the city's ban on carry outside the home to be unconstitutional.

The city adopted an incredibly restrictive ordinance governing concealed carry in the District, which was subsequently challenged by SAF in a second case, *Wrenn v. District of Columbia.*

The way carry cases are being addressed by the courts underscores the importance of federal elections. The president makes appointments to the federal bench, including the Supreme Court. The Senate ratifies those appointments. If an anti-gun liberal is in the White House, and the Senate is controlled by his/her party, the courts can be stacked for years with anti-gun federal judges who, despite two high court rulings, stubbornly refuse to accept the concept that the right to keep and *bear* arms is a fundamental individual civil right. Only be getting rid of such judges and replacing them with jurists who understand and accept the full meaning of the Founders who wrote the Second Amendment will this issue ever be fully resolved.

Making the case in court

Of the many court victories supporting the right to carry, one that is particularly dear to Second Amendment advocates is *Moore v. Madigan*, the common name applied to actually two cases – one filed by the Second Amendment Foundation and the other by the National Rifle Association – that forced the State of Illinois to adopt a concealed carry statute. This case and the ruling that came out of it was discussed briefly in Chapter One. Until this pair of cases, the Prairie State legislature and its anti-gun governor had stubbornly refused to consider legislation allowing concealed carry, making Illinois the only state in the nation that did not have such a law on the books.

Moore v. Madigan was the SAF case, while the NRA's litigation was known as *Shepard v. Madigan*. When the two cases were heard by the Seventh Circuit Court of Appeals at the same time, they were identified by the initial *Moore* case as is customary in the courts when two similar cases are heard together.

To refresh your memory, the appellate court's decision infuriated Illinois anti-gunners and sent a shockwave through the gun prohibition community. It forced lawmakers in Springfield to adopt a "shall issue" law that then-Gov. Pat Quinn tried to change, but was overruled by the legislature. Writing for the majority, Judge Richard Posner noted that "Confrontations are not limited to the home." His observation that "a Chicagoan is a good deal more likely to be attacked on a sidewalk in a rough neighborhood than in his apartment on the 35th floor of the Park Tower" was akin to poking the liberal establishment in the ribs with a pointed stick. Posner's common sense analysis brought groans from the gun prohibition crowd, but to no avail. The decision stood, and an appeal to the Supreme Court was rendered unnecessary when the legislature took over and passed the carry law.

Up in Michigan as this book was being written, another carry case was in the courts, having initially been decided in favor of an armed citizen named Kenneth Herman and Michigan Open Carry, an activist group. They had sued the Clio School District because Herman had been repeatedly denied access to his daughter's elementary school because he habitually carries a sidearm openly. State law allows concealed carry in schools, but open carry is another matter, or so the district maintained.

But Circuit Judge Archie Hayman came down on Herman's side. As this book was being written, an appeal was likely.

The one thing about court victories that must keep in perspective is that they can become defeats on appeal.

Such was the case in Maryland that began as *Woollard v. Sheridan*, which became *Woollard v. Gallagher* on appeal. This was a promising case because it struck at the very heart of so-called "discretionary carry" statutes that allow law enforcement and/or bureaucrats to arbitrarily determine who does, or does not, get a carry license.

The case involved Raymond Woollard, the victim of a home invasion by his then son-in-law, Kris Lee Abbott. Following that incident, Woollard was granted a concealed carry permit by Maryland authorities in 2003, and it was renewed in 2006. But when he applied for renewal a second time, in 2009, the application was rejected because he had not "submitted any documentation to verify threats occurring beyond his residence, where he can already legally carry a handgun." It was an astonishing turn of events because by that time, Abbott had been released from prison and he was living not far from the Woollard home.

The Second Amendment Foundation sued with attorney Alan Gura – the winning attorney in both the *Heller* and *McDonald* Supreme Court cases – handling the case. At the trial level, District Judge Benson Everett Legg issued an opinion that matter-of-factly threw cold water on the Maryland statute.

As quoted by a SAF press release printed by Ammoland, Judge Legg noted, "In addition to self-defense, the (Second Amendment) right was also understood to allow for militia membership and hunting. To secure these rights, the Second Amendment's protections must extend beyond the home: neither hunting nor militia training is a household activity, and 'self-defense has to take place wherever [a] person happens to be'."

"A citizen may not be required to offer a 'good and substantial reason' why he should be permitted to exercise his rights," Judge Legg additionally noted. "The right's existence is all the reason he needs."

Makes sense, right? Well, not to the Fourth Circuit Court of Appeals. As noted in the Wikipedia history of the case, the Fourth Circuit unanimously reversed Judge Legg's ruling. Subsequently, the Supreme Court declined to hear an appeal, so the reversal stands.

But wait! That opinion stands in the Fourth Circuit. A few hundred miles to the south, in the State of Florida, a different ruling by the Florida state Court of Appeals in a case known as *Norman v. State*, provides another perspective.

As explained by Eugene Volokh in his "Volokh Conspiracy" blog for the *Washington Post*, the Florida appeals court ruled that the Second Amendment protects carry of firearms for personal protection outside the home. While the Maryland statute doesn't exactly ban the carrying of defensive sidearms outside the home, the way the law is administered amounts to a restriction of the highest nature.

As Volokh observed, "...the court rejected the view of some federal circuits (the Second, Third, and Fourth) that highly restrictive licensing schemes, under which applicants must satisfy law enforcement that they have particular self-defense needs (rather than just the normal self-defense needs of the public at large) before they can get a license."

Volokh quickly added that the court in Florida observed that legislative discretion "in this area is not limitless." He then noted problems in other states and federal court districts, specifically mentioning the Woollard case as an example.

What was interesting about the Norman case was that the court upheld restrictions on open carry. Florida is a strong concealed carry state, but because licenses to carry are issued for concealed carry, the court reasoned that a restriction on open carry is allowed.

Volokh, who is highly respected in the firearms community, stated, "I think the court was quite right to recognize a right to carry guns in public for self-defense. I also think the court was right to allow the state to limit such carrying to concealed carrying, precisely because such carrying doesn't substantially interfere with the ability to defend oneself."

Wisdom from the bench

Whatever else these carry cases accomplish, they allow for some learned wisdom from the bench, and sometimes not. They also demonstrate the importance of which people are appointed to the bench and who appoints them.

In early 2014, a divided U.S. 9th Circuit Court of Appeals panel issued a split decision on concealed carry permit regulations in several California jurisdictions including Los Angeles, San Francisco, San Diego and Orange County. Two of the judges were appointed by Republican presidents and the dissenting judge was a Bill Clinton appointee. The decision was described by the *Los Angeles Times* as "a significant victory for gun owners."

This was the case of *Peruta v. San Diego*. Writing for the majority, Judge Diarmuid O'Scannlain – a Reagan appointee – observed, "We are not holding that the Second Amendment requires the states to permit concealed carry. But the Second Amendment does require that the states permit some form of carry for self-defense outside the home."

At issue was the requirement of permit applicants to show a "need" to carry a firearm in public. This is generically called "the good need" or "justifiable need" restriction that amounts to an excuse for not issuing a permit.

At about the same time, a Second Amendment Foundation/Calguns Foundation case known as *Richards v. Prieto* also scored a victory in the Ninth Circuit. This was a challenge to the handgun carry license issuing policy of Yolo County, California Sheriff Ed Prieto. The initial ruling against the plaintiffs was reversed and remanded.

The Richards case was argued at the same time, and before the same panel, that earlier decided NRA's *Peruta case*. Yolo County and Sheriff Prieto had argued that their policies were distinguishable from those struck down in Peruta, but the three-judge panel unanimously disagreed.

In both cases, California's "may issue" regulation was on the line. Because of the disparity between the Ninth Circuit and the other circuits over the issue of discretionary (and arbitrary) carry permit laws, right-to-carry proponents frustrated by earlier reluctance by the Supreme Court to hear a case that once and for all would decide that the right to bear arms extends beyond the front door to someone's home were looking at Richards and Peruta with cautious optimism.

But that optimism was crushed when the en banc panel of the Ninth Circuit ruled against *Peruta*. The court's 7-4 majority ruling was astonishing to many in the Second Amendment community because the court bluntly said, "there is no Second Amendment right for members of the general public to carry concealed firearms in public."

The decision underscored the importance of election outcomes. Federal judges and Supreme Court justices are nominated by the president and confirmed by the Senate. But the language in the *Peruta* ruling also raised a question the court did not answer. If concealed carry is not protected, does that mean the Constitution protects open carry? There are only two ways to "bear" arms: openly or concealed.

The bottom line here is that the Supreme Court needs to get off its reluctance and settle this the only way that the issue can be settled: Affirmatively for gun owners, and they know it.

All together now: "A civil right that is limited in its exercise only to the confines of one's home is not a civil right at all, but a restrictively regulated government privilege."

The right to keep and bear arms is a fundamental civil right protected by the Second Amendment. We take civil rights everywhere, to the bank, grocery store, shopping mall, gas station, theater, concert hall, restaurant, public park, national forest, ocean beach, campground, university campus, hospital and even city hall; perhaps especially city hall and the state legislature.

Many Second Amendment advocates consider it an outrage that the high court has let stand what they believe are egregious infringements on the right to bear arms. Among those was the law in New Jersey that requires gun owners to demonstrate a justifiable need in order to carry firearms in public. This was the *Drake case*, supported by SAF and the Association of New Jersey Rifle and Pistol Clubs. This was a case before the 3rd U.S. Circuit Court of Appeals, in which the panel upheld the opinion of U.S. District Judge William Walls that issuing permits to most if not all applicants – as is done in states with "shall issue" requirements – would essentially satisfy "the subjective need based on nothing more than 'general fears' to go about their daily lives prepared to use deadly force. The risks associated with a judicial error in discouraging regulation of firearms carried in public are too great," as noted in one published report.

One could presumably argue that there is no verifiable data to suggest that legally-armed private citizens pose any greater threat to community peace and tranquility

In another disappointing ruling, this one from the 10th U.S. Circuit Court of Appeals in a 2013 case known as *Peterson v. Martinez*, the court ruled that there really is no Second Amendment right to carry a concealed firearm in public. This was a case involving a Washington State resident, Gray Peterson, who was challenging the Colorado law that only allowed issuance of concealed carry permits to state residents, and it does not honor Washington's concealed pistol license.

This is one of those cases that might best serve as a warning that sometimes even cases with the best of intentions can result in far more than one bargained for. In its ruling against Peterson, the court wrote, "In light of our nation's extensive practice of restricting citizens' freedom to carry firearms in a concealed manner, we hold that this activity does not fall within the scope of the Second Amendment's protections."

And then there was this, which underscores the need for the Supreme Court to take up the question of carrying guns outside the home: "Given that the concealed carrying of firearms has not been recognized as a right, and the fact that concealed carry was prohibited for resident and non-resident alike for much of our history, we cannot declare this activity sufficiently basic to the livelihood of the Nation."

Some might scratch their heads and wonder aloud, "What the hell happened?"

That might best be explained by how this case, and its loss, was reported and analyzed by The Blaze. While recognizing Peterson's personal dilemma of being unable to carry openly in Denver, where that is prohibited by city ordinance, and unable to obtain a concealed handgun license because he was a non-resident, *The Blaze* observed that "when it comes to the Second Amendment, the right to keep and bear arms is far less absolute than many people might like to think."

A couple of paragraphs later, the publication noted, "For now, at least, the legal reality regarding the Second Amendment is that it does guarantee a right to keep and bear arms of some kind to individual citizens. Barring a massive shift in power on the court, this is unlikely to change, as five of the sitting justices voted to hold that the right exists and protects citizens against both state and federal law..."

Challenging emergency powers

Further illustrating just how different courts act in different jurisdictions is the North Carolina case of *Bateman v. Purdue*, another SAF case, this one filed in cooperation with Grass Roots North Carolina and three individual plaintiffs. At issue was the state's emergency powers act that banned firearms and ammunition outside the home during a declared emergency. That could include anything from a hurricane to some man-made problem, such as a riot or terrorist act.

At times like that, people might very well need a firearm and ammunition outside the home simply to survive.

When SAF and its allies won that case, the ruling handed down by U.S. District Judge Malcolm J. Howard was to the point regarding the right to bear arms outside the home.

"While the bans imposed pursuant to these statutes may be limited in duration," Judge Howard wrote, "it cannot be overlooked that the statutes strip peaceable, law abiding citizens of the right to arm themselves in defense of hearth and home, striking at the very core of the Second Amendment."

The judge explained that the Supreme Court in *Heller* noted that the right to keep and bear arms "was valued not only for preserving the militia, but 'more important(ly) for self-defense and hunting."

"Therefore," Judge Malcolm observed, "the Second Amendment right to keep and bear arms 'is not strictly limited to the home environment but extends in some form to wherever those activities or needs occur…

"Under the laws at issue here, citizens are prohibited from engaging, outside their home, in any activities secured by the Second Amendment," he explained. "They may not carry defensive weapons outside the home, hunt or engage in firearm related sporting activities. Additionally, although the statutes do not *directly* regulate the possession of firearms within the home, they effectively prohibit law abiding citizens from purchasing and transporting to their homes firearms and ammunition needed for self-defense. As such, these laws burden conduct protected by the Second Amendment."

Two months later, the state decided not to appeal the case.

Out in Washington, a state-level case involving a man charged with openly carrying firearms was decided by the state court of appeals with some surprising language. While the ruling in *State v. Gregory Casad* was unpublished, it set a common-sense tone that other courts have paid attention to, along with several state lawmakers and other public officials.

Casad's case dates back to 2005, when a woman called police on him for carrying what appeared to be a rifle wrapped in a purple towel. While not expressing concern for her safety, she told authorities that "it just looked kind of suspicious to me," according to court documents.

Washington, like many other states, recognizes and allows open carry under its state constitution. When the case was finally decided by the appellate court, here's what the unanimous opinion, written by the late Judge Christine Quinn-Brintnall noted:

> "We note that, in connection with this case, several individuals have commented that they would find it strange, maybe shocking, to see a man carrying a gun down the street in broad daylight. Casad's appellate counsel conceded that she would personally react with shock, but she emphasized that an individual's lack of comfort with firearms does not equate to reasonable alarm. We agree. It is not unlawful for a person to responsibly walk down the

street with a visible firearm, even if this action would shock some people."

Court conflicts

Among the more perplexing problems facing Second Amendment advocates is how to explain to journalists that the Second Amendment doesn't "create" anything. In a prescient column written back in 2013 for *Time* magazine, Adam Cohen accurately predicted the next gun control battle to be fought in the courts would be over right to carry in public places.

Yet Cohen stated, "In 2008, the Supreme Court overturned a lot of accepted wisdom about gun control when it ruled in District Columbia v. Heller that the Second Amendment creates an individual right to possess a firearm. Until then, it was widely – if not universally – believed that the amendment was about raising 'a well-regulated militia' – not about guaranteeing individuals the right to carry a gun."

This followed the Peterson case in Colorado, discussed earlier in this chapter. Cohen noted that, while a court in Denver was going one direction, another case was getting a different ruling in the 7th Circuit Court of Appeals in Chicago. That was the attempt to set aside the ruling by Judge Posner in the Moore case, detailed a few pages back.

The problem is that some judges and a lot of attorneys contend that the Second Amendment created or granted some right, so they act accordingly.

Perhaps the most important thing Cohen stated was that, "The conflicting Denver and Chicago rulings underscore just how uncertain gun law is now." No truer words were ever put on paper, for it must be abundantly clear that when it comes to the Second Amendment, the legal ground is still being plowed, and many courts seem rather reluctant to make rulings they worry might be later overturned, or that run counter to the dogma to which they have subscribed.

Even with conflicting opinions between the circuits, the Supreme Court at this writing still was turning down cases with lots of potential. And Cohen addressed this problem by asking, "Does the Second Amendment simply confer a right to have a gun at home? Does it mean there is a right to have a gun in public – but that states can still ban *concealed* weapons? Does it prohibit complete bans on concealed weapons – but allow more narrowly drawn ones, such as a requirement that people get permits to carry concealed weapons? Or does it, as some gun-rights advocates believe, bar any restrictions on carrying guns – in home or on the street, in the open or concealed?

"It is unlikely that Second Amendment law will end up in such an extreme position – and it should not," he added. "It is one thing to say that there is a constitutional right to keep a gun at home for protection. It is quite another to say there is a constitutional right to bring a hidden gun into a daycare center. Even though the Supreme Court has expanded the Second Amendment, there is little reason to believe it will take it that far."

But why not? Why would the high court not acknowledge and rule – like it or not – that the right to *bear* arms applies to all kinds of places, including areas that gun prohibitionists would have us consider taboo to firearms? As earlier noted, one does not park his or

12: RIGHT TO CARRY BUT NOT OFFEND

"Nobody has the right to not be offended. That right doesn't exist in any declaration I have ever read." – Salman Rushdie

"I hate rude behavior in a man. I won't tolerate it." – Woodrow F. Call, fictional character in 'Lonesome Dove'

Responsibility. It comes with every civil right whether some of us like that or not, and those who abuse their exercise of any right with boorish behavior do no credit to the right, or to anyone else who exercises it.

Salman Rushdie, the British-Indian novelist who offended a lot of people with his fourth novel, *The Satanic Verses*, to the point that his death was called for by the Muslim leadership in Iran many years ago, once observed, "If you are offended it is your problem, and frankly lots of things offend lots of people."

That so many gun prohibitionists are offended by the thought – not necessarily the actual sight but just the thought – of an armed citizen leaves them looking rather silly when one has the opportunity to analyze what those people are saying. The actual sight of a firearm on a citizen's hip sends some anti-gunners into emotional orbit, and the mere thought that there might be thousands of armed citizens with *concealed* sidearms makes them shudder. We discussed this earlier, in Chapter Four.

While there is no rational justification for harboring such a visceral objection to the open carry of a firearm in a peaceable manner by a private citizen, there is another side of that equation, and it is one that some gun activists can't seem to understand. There is, according to many political activists in the firearms community, also no justification for playing in-your-face politics with firearms as your props, especially long guns, just to demonstrate that you can do it. Critics of the practice say that serves no constructive purpose, and – at least in Washington State in early 2015 – it actually had the negative effect of getting open carry of any firearm banned inside the House and Senate chambers of the state capitol building.

It is still legal to carry concealed (when done properly, who really knows?) and presumably lots of Second Amendment proponents do so, but open carry was prohibited after about two dozen people attending a gun rights rally on the state capitol steps in Olympia during that year's legislative session broke away from the main group and walked inside with long guns, some of which were being carried at what firearms enthusiasts call "low ready," with muzzles aimed toward the floor and off to one side, both hands on the gun, fingers off the trigger.

Some of those involved and their supporters argued that the problem was with the anti-gun legislative leadership, while other gun rights activists said the problem clearly was with the demonstrators. You be the judge.

Down in Texas, some open carry advocates with two groups calling themselves DontComply.com and Come and Take It Texas conducted what they called a "mock mass shooting" near the campus of the University of Texas at Austin. Originally, the "drill" was to have been conducted on campus property, but university officials nixed that idea quickly, so the event was moved to property near the campus. This event came only days after the San Bernardino terrorist attack, and many people considered it in rather bad taste.

The event was staged as a protest against so-called "gun free zones," but it soon devolved into a political football event when the group Students for Concealed Carry (SCC) denounced the idea. That group, and Texas pro-gunners had successfully lobbied for legislation allowing campus carry, and they viewed the event as counter-productive. Texas gun rights activists had also pushed through an open carry law.

Those victories came after hard-fought battles that occurred over the course of years, and proponents were in no mood to have a couple of small activist groups give anyone in the legislature reason to reconsider.

In a scathing press release, Antonia Okafor, SCC Southwest regional director stated, "I'm astounded that eighteen months after most of the state's open carry groups figured out that carrying rifles and shotguns into restaurants and grocery stores isn't a solid public-relations strategy, one such group apparently thinks that introducing openly carried long guns, fake blood, and the sound of gunshots into a university community that is highly uncertain about the new campus carry law and understandably concerned about recent high-profile mass shootings is a smart idea."

The *Austin newspaper* quoted UT history professor Joan Neuberger, who is also associated with a group called Gun Free UT that opposed campus carry. She was just as critical.

"Staging a mass shooting during an anxious time for students — finals week — not only breaks rules but shows real disrespect for the feelings of students, faculty and staff who don't want to have guns around them in the first place, but will be forced to put up with guns in public places in 2016," she told the newspaper.

A spokesman for organizers of the "Open Carry Walk and Crisis Performance" event, Matthew Short, told the Austin newspaper that "Criminals that want to do evil things and commit murder go places where people are not going to be able to stop them. When seconds count, the cops are minutes away." He maintained that so many people were killed in San Bernardino because nobody was allowed to be armed.

It was one of those "Just because you *can* do something doesn't mean you *should* do it" situations.

Virginia back-and-forth

Just as one person's boorish behavior is another person's protest for liberty, so also are executive actions by anti-gun politicians considered grand ideas by some and treachery by others. Late in 2015, when there was lots of talk about the president taking executive action on guns, state-level politicians seemed intent on following his lead.

It happened in Virginia, where Democrat Attorney General Mark R. Herring announced just before Christmas that the state would be dropping its recognition of concealed carry permits and licenses from 25 other states. Anti-gun Virginia Gov. Terry McAuliffe had earlier prohibited the open carrying of sidearms in executive branch offices and government buildings, and Herring's action seemed to many people to be his effort to rub salt into an open wound.

In its coverage of the story, the *Washington Post* said Herring had been reviewing reciprocity agreements the Commonwealth had with 30 other states. He claimed that 25 states had weaker concealed handgun carry laws than Virginia's, so those states' permits or licenses were no longer recognized.

What the exercise did, of course, was swipe at the self-defense rights of law-abiding citizens who may be visiting Virginia. As a result, several of those states stopped recognizing Virginia permits. Every action has an equal and opposite reaction.

Weeks later, of course, McAuliffe reversed course by reaching an agreement with gun rights activists, and signed legislation that nullified Herring's move. Virginia will recognize out-of-state permits and licenses in exchange for restrictions on prohibited persons.

This sort of political gamesmanship by Herring does nothing to put a dent in crime, but it does help perpetuate the practice of discrimination by liberals against firearms owners. It maintains the mindset that gun rights are subject to government restriction and revocation.

Over the past couple of years, there has been another strategy designed solely to harass honest gun owners. It's called "swatting" and involves what are essentially false reports to police about crimes that result in the deployment of special teams to the addresses of gun owners.

When the Coalition to Stop Gun Violence (CSGV) went on social media urging people to call police if they see someone carrying a gun, it caused no small amount of angst among legally-armed people who did not care to be treated like criminals. As reported by Fox News, the Coalition message was rather alarmist.

"If you see someone carrying a firearm in public—openly or concealed—and have ANY doubts about their intent, call 911 immediately and ask police to come to the scene," the Coalition said on its Facebook page. "Never put your safety, or the safety of your loved ones, at the mercy of weak gun laws that arm individuals in public with little or no criminal and/or mental health screening."

This message served only to perpetuate the stereotype of a gun owner as a dangerous loon and to create fear as a reflex response to the sight of an open-carrier. What other purpose could there have been? That sort of harassment-by-proxy may be popular to laugh about at cocktail parties, but it is also a falsehood that could create all sorts of problems for the gun owner, even to the point of getting him or her mistakenly killed by an overzealous police officer.

The Fox News report asserted that this was not the first time that the CSGV "and other gun control advocates" had done such a thing. Fox recalled a *National Review* article from October 2014 in which writer Charles C.W. Cooke reported that supporters of anti-gun groups had encouraged people to "call the police and intentionally exaggerate what they see in hopes of getting cops to stop those open-carrying guns."

Had some harm come to anyone as a result of this intentional harassment, there could have been potential criminal charges. Genuine alarm is one thing. Needlessly exaggerating alarm, or inventing it out of whole cloth, is quite another.

The Dallas O.C. incident

On the other hand – and honest Second Amendment advocates will acknowledge there is an "other hand" in this equation – some activists have been known to push the envelope. Over and above what occurred near the University of Texas campus in Austin, described at the beginning of this chapter, there have been incidents involving gun activists that had less than stellar results.

We already discussed the disastrous political fallout from the open carry incident in Olympia, Washington in early 2015 that resulted in a prohibition on openly carried firearms in the Senate and House public viewer galleries.

An incident at a Dallas, Texas Chipotle restaurant in 2014 involving members of one local open carry advocacy group became a "poster child" event. Several people entered the restaurant carrying long guns, which admittedly at the time was the only type of gun that could legally be openly carried in Texas. But what was accomplished?

Chipotle quickly asked customers to not bring loaded long guns into its establishments. It played right into the hands, and the anti-gun agenda, of Moms Demand Action for Gun Sense in America. And, to be candid, it apparently frightened some people.

ABC News did a story about the activities of Open Carry Texas (OCT), reporting that "a group of gun-carrying activists in Texas...brazenly flex their legal right to bear arms by carrying around assault rifles in public. The group calls themselves 'Open Carry Texas.' Their enthusiasm for packing heat in public has led national chains like Chipotle, Chili's and Jack in the Box to ask customers to leave their firearms at home."

The network immediately acknowledged that, "What the group is doing is perfectly legal in Texas, but they have come to represent the line in the sand between those in America who fear the violent use of guns and those who fear losing their guns."

The story also said that OCT had set as its mission to "raise awareness of existing gun rights" and to expand those rights. Among Texas gun rights advocates, there is some disagreement whether the OCT's activities were responsible for, or perhaps slowed the process of passing the state's open carry law. That debate may continue, but it is now something of a moot point, since open carry has been legalized in the Lone Star State.

When *Slate* published a 2013 piece on the open carry movement, it cited an incident in Texas at which some 40 open carriers showed up outside a restaurant where members of the anti-gun Moms Demand Action for Gun Sense in America, an organization associated with Michael Bloomberg's Everytown for Gun Safety lobbying group, were meeting. The article said Moms members were alarmed.

"Whether or not open-carry counterdemonstrations are a good thing," the article observed, "they are assuredly a thing. Opponents of gun control strap on weapons and parade around to prove that parading around with weapons is constitutional and that they have a First Amendment right to say so. They increasingly target other meetings for these demonstrations. Open-carry advocates demonstrated at an MDA event in Indianapolis last spring and at a Let's Roll America event on the Texas capitol grounds last month. This goes beyond the open-carry demonstration at the site of John F. Kennedy's assassination in Dallas or the open-carry protest at the Alamo in October. What we are seeing is new: These are demonstrations that target gun-control activists at their meetings and demonstrations that attempt to provoke the police into responding. By that definition they are expressive First Amendment activity. The question is whether that activity can and should be limited."

It was not the first time a franchise chain had asked people to leave their guns at home if they planned to visit. Starbucks took a lot of heat over open carry, and the franchise seemed okay with simply telling the public that it complied with local regulations. The company was neither for nor against the legal carry of firearms in its franchises.

But some people pushed their luck, staging open carry "appreciation" events or other gatherings at some stores. This resulted in the famous appeal from Starbucks CEO Howard Schultz in 2013 to gun owners that they not bring their guns inside. It was not a ban, as gun prohibitionists tried to portray it, but it was more than just a signal that some folks had carried things too far and it was time to cool their jets.

As Schultz explained in the open letter to his "fellow Americans," Starbucks employees did not want to be thrust into the middle of the gun debate. All Starbucks wants to do is serve customers and make a profit, not become a political football.

All of these anecdotal incidents bring us around to where this discussion inevitably has to go: If the behavior is lawful, who can justifiably criticize it?

Shift the discussion to an annual event in the far left-leaning city of Seattle, where there is a naked bike ride conducted at the Fremont neighborhood Solstice celebration. This is hardly a sanctioned event, having started some years ago when, according to a short history on Wikipedia, "streakers...crashed the parade." The parade and celebration is an event put on by the Fremont Arts Council, but the naked bike ride is the handiwork of the Solstice Cyclists, also known as "The Painted [Naked] Cyclists of the Solstice Parade."

It's turned into something of a bizarre activity that draws some laughs, some sneers, and a few television cameras. Instead of simply riding in the buff, participants now show up with various sorts of body painting. According to Wikipedia, "The group is the largest and fastest growing ensemble associated with the parade."

There are laws against lewd conduct, covering public nudity, but it seems to be an exception in Seattle to tolerate the naked bike ride.

On the other hand, open carry in Seattle, which is not simply protected by law but by the state constitution, gets a far different reaction. Some, though certainly not all, open carriers in the Jet City have occasionally found themselves in conversations with Seattle police officers over the years.

Maybe if the open carriers just wore gunbelts and holsters, and nothing else, there would be a happy compromise. They could explain to critics that there is simply no way to conceal a sidearm if one is prancing around in the altogether.

The proverbial "bottom line" is the fact that nobody has been harmed by the naked bike ride, and the same can be said of open carry. There is no evidence that any harm has come to anyone because someone else happened to be openly carrying a firearm in a peaceable manner. Any emotional discomfort suffered by people who have a reflexive fear of the sight of a gun is *their* problem, and nobody else's.

Open Carry blunt talk

Two respected names in the firearms community are Massad Ayoob and Tom Gresham. Ayoob is the nationally-famous author and self-defense expert whose byline has graced just about every firearms periodical on the newsstands, and who has appeared as an expert witness in several criminal trials. He was the founder of the Lethal Force Institute, and now operates a self-defense training enterprise called the Massad Ayoob Group.

Gresham is the award-winning host and founder of *Gun Talk Radio*, a syndicated radio program broadcast nationally on Sundays. He has a reputation for candor and honesty, and he is not afraid to challenge anyone in the firearms community, or the gun control lobby.

Long story short, when these guys talk, people listen.

When Ayoob, writing in his *Backwoods Home* blog, addressed open carry, he was blunt and perhaps a bit abrasive because he expressed some opinions that raised eyebrows. In the process he may have snapped some over-enthusiastic open carry activists back into some semblance of reality.

"The gains the gun owners' civil rights movement have made can be attributed to decades of legal scholarship," he observed, "working within the system, and reforming anti-gun laws which largely trace back to anti-black bias in the antebellum and Reconstruction-era south, anti-immigrant bias in the industrialized north, and culture war at multiple levels.

"Gun-banners will never convert most who read this blog," Ayoob added, "and we who support a responsibly armed citizenry will never win over the (Nancy) Pelosis and (Michael) Bloombergs of the world. The battleground lies with the vast majority of people who are in the middle on this polarized issue. I am old enough to remember when Massachusetts and California each held a referendum on whether possession of handguns should be banned in their states. Neither state had a majority of gun owners in the voting pool, but in each case our side won the referendum, because 'the people on the fence' didn't want to go that far.

"Doing things that alarm those people in the middle will do nothing to help the pro-gun side," he stated. "Fear is the key ingredient that creates hatred. Doing things that put the general public in fear will cause more people to hate us, and anyone who seriously thinks flaunting rifles around schools in cities and suburbs will somehow acclimate the public to an acceptance of armed citizens is simply delusional."

WHAM! In three paragraphs, Ayoob put boorish behavior with firearms as political props into its proper perspective. Of course, some hardcore absolutists might disagree, defending their own conduct, but for the average gun owner and many non-gun owners, there was logic to his assessment and criticism. And he didn't stop there.

"Please, don't compare the heavily armed guy who video-records himself confronting police to Rosa Parks on a segregated bus," he explained. "Ms. Parks did not put anyone in fear of their lives. Don't tell me that 'a right not exercised is a right denied,' when we've seen confrontational open carry result in stricter laws in California, and hamper the responsible open carry movement in Texas much more recently."

This column was a follow-up to something Ayoob had written a few days earlier at *Backwoods Home*. In that piece, he had unabashedly and unapologetically referred to in-your-face open carry as "the province of those colloquially known as 'attention whores'."

He noted elsewhere in that piece that, "I don't think we win any friends for gun owners' civil rights by flaunting deadly weapons in the face of a general public conditioned to fear guns and their owners by generations of anti-gun media and political prejudice."

Ayoob was hardly trying to dismiss open carry, as a practice or a movement. But he clearly discerned between prudent conduct and what might be considered misconduct. He noted that he occasionally open carries "just to gauge typical response," and he said the majority of people he encountered "don't even notice."

Therein lays the key: It's not that someone engages in an unusual practice, it is the manner in which they engage that makes the difference.

Meanwhile, Gresham writes an on-line blog called "The Truth Squad." In one of his columns, he looked at open carry and compared some of the activism to the gay rights movement and the campaign for women's rights.

"Rights, like muscles, must be exercised," he wrote. "To not use open carry is to lose that right. If the police are restricting and arresting people for engaging in a legal act, we have a serious problem. You and I may differ in our opinions as to whether carrying a gun openly is smart from a tactical sense, but that's a different issue. OCM, as a 'movement,' now has achieved the position that concealed carry had 20 years ago, except that the battle then was to get carry laws passed. Many states do not prohibit open carry, so the movement is to get more people to do it, and to change the laws so good people can open carry in more states."

Later in his column, Gresham observed, "If you decide to carry openly, you must know the laws. It would be a good idea to carry a copy of the applicable laws in the event you are confronted about it...Learn how they handle the questions and even the visits by police officers who often don't know that open carry is legal. One hopes not to run into an officer who, like the one in Louisiana, would say, 'I don't care if it's legal, if you do it here, you'll get arrested.' That's a policy which will cost the city a lot of money.

"Why get involved in the OCM," he concluded. "Why carry openly? Comfort? Making a point? Just to exercise a right, perhaps? All valid reasons, in my opinion. Maybe it's just one person's way to show others that good people carry guns. It might not be for everyone, but it's a movement that's growing..."

Were Ayoob and Gresham on opposite sides of the debate? Not at all. Both men recognize the practice of open carry. They just believe people who do it must act with prudence and use common sense.

And therein is the key to all debates about firearms. People who use and carry them responsibly are sort of like ambassadors for the Second Amendment. Others who use or carry firearms irresponsibly are no friends to the gun rights movement, and they just might become the examples anti-gunners frequently point to in an effort to portray all armed citizens as louts whose rights need to be heavily regulated.

Terror changes everything

In August 2015, prior to the terrorist attacks in Paris, San Bernardino, Brussels and Orlando that ignited a rush to gun shops and sporting goods stores by people, many of whom had never before owned a gun much less considered carrying one for personal protection, Fox News did a story about concealed carry in Detroit, Michigan. The focus was somewhat on Police Chief James Craig, an outspoken proponent of personal defense by legally-armed private citizens.

In that story, Fox discussed a local resident identified as Darrell Standberry, who is licensed to carry and proclaimed that, "I never leave home without my weapon." He had to use that gun one night when a car thief – a convicted felon with a lengthy criminal record and gun he could not legally possess – tried to steal Standberry's car. Attempting to add insult to injury, the thug didn't just drive away, he turned the SUV around and tried to run down Standberry, drawing his illegally-carried gun in the process.

Tough luck for the bad guy because Standberry drew his own .45-caliber Sig Sauer semi-auto pistol and fatally shot the man. It was a textbook case of self-defense.

What this man did was necessary to defend his own life. That is hardly offensive conduct with a firearm. That's ultimately what carrying a defensive sidearm is all about. Anyone offended by what Standberry did is simply looking for an excuse to be offended.

Detroit Chief Craig, the Fox story explained, had encouraged citizens in that city to be proactive about their personal safety. Crime was up, the police force was shrinking because of a shrinking economy, and the career lawman who had worked in several other jurisdictions made it clear that this was a "call to arms."

The story said local firearms instructors had been a busy bunch. Thousands of Detroit citizens have handguns, and they were obviously serious about defending themselves and following the chief's advice.

Much of Detroit's population is African-American, and according to Fox, they are a huge part of the city's "growing embrace of Second Amendment rights." In a sense, this is a pure definition of the term "black lives matter." Chief Craig, by the way, is also African-American.

A Pew Research poll cited by Fox revealed that 54 percent of African-Americans support legal gun ownership for personal protection. Is there something surprising about that? Being conscious of one's own safety and the safety of their families and homes isn't color-exclusive. The late Otis McDonald, the gentle-spoken man at the center of the landmark Chicago handgun ban case decided by the U.S. Supreme Court in 2010, was also African-American, and so is Rhonda Ezell, the central figure in the case challenging Chicago's ultra-restrictive handgun ordinance that tried to prohibit the development of gun ranges inside the city limits.

Self-defense is a universal *human* right, perhaps the oldest right of all. It's the right of self-preservation, and there is not a jurisdiction anywhere in the United States that does not recognize this right, although some have placed incredibly tight restraints on its exercise.

In Detroit, as elsewhere across the country, people don't necessarily want to ever use a handgun in self-defense, but growing numbers have decided that if they ever *need* one, they better *have* one.

That brings us around to Trevor Hughes, the Denver-based correspondent for *USA Today* who publicly declared in a holiday-week column that he had, "after months of soul-searching," decided to purchase a handgun. Perhaps revealing something about the anti-gun mindset in far too many newspaper editorial offices and news rooms, he noted that, "At least one co-worker came near to tears as she tried to dissuade me."

Too bad, lady, because it's Trevor's life at stake, perhaps, not yours. And Trevor appears to have determined that his life is worth something.

What Hughes called his "tipping point" was the same thing that moved many other non-gun owners off the political fence, or across it, to the retail counters of gun shops and sporting goods stores across the country. The terrorist attack in San Bernardino on Dec. 7 – a date that will live in infamy – told America that the nation is not immune. Assurances from authorities that there are "no credible" indications an attack may be coming have lost their credibility.

There was no small amount of solid reasoning in what Hughes wrote, particularly this passage, which seems to provide a summation about why increasing numbers of law-abiding Americans are packing heat:

"But if me carrying a concealed weapon — just like millions of my responsible neighbors in this country — deters someone from attacking my friends and neighbors, maybe that's worth it. You don't see terror attacks in this country on areas where there's lots of armed men and women. Instead, it's those soft targets that get hit. Maybe it's time we made sure our enemies, both foreign and domestic, understand that we shoot back."

That's a principle not only terrorists but street thugs, home invaders and other criminals should also be reminded of frequently.

Following the San Bernardino attack, several law enforcement officials around the country openly encouraged citizens in their jurisdictions to carry firearms legally if they had licenses or permits. One could almost hear the wails from anti-gunners who had long relied on police chiefs and sheriffs to act as props for their gun control efforts. That worm has turned.

Perhaps no better example of this was a message the police chief in the town of Sedro Woolley, Washington posted on Facebook. Sedro Woolley is a community of about 11,000 on the banks of the Skagit River about 90 miles north of Seattle, and possibly at the opposite end of the political universe.

Chief Lin Tucker, in a conversation with author Workman, said that many gun control advocates are "not terribly well educated."

"They want to reach out for something to solve a problem," he surmised. "Guns are easy (targets)."

Tucker, a self-described NRA member since his teens, with a background that includes having been a firearms instructor, is a career law enforcement professional. He understands the difference between lawfully-armed citizens and miscreants, and he noted that honest people obey the law while criminals ignore it.

His personally-written advice to armed citizens on the department's Facebook page elicited scores of responses, all but one of which were positive. He advised armed citizens to "be aware of your surroundings" and to "Think before introducing a firearm into a potentially volatile situation."

He cautioned against carrying a gun while drinking alcohol, and especially to know basic firearms safety rules. Translation: "Treat all firearms as if they were loaded."

"Don't point your weapon at anything you are not willing to kill or destroy," Chief Tucker cautioned, and "Be sure of your backstop and what is beyond it."

Importantly, he encouraged people to "Think about why you want to carry a firearm and what type of scenario would prompt you to draw your weapon. Then think, would it be better for all involved if I was an excellent witness and called 911 or is there an immediate threat to someone's safety and there's no reasonably effective alternative to using force???"

Exercise discretion

No civil right is unlimited. "Shall not be infringed" does not mean people can be careless or negligent with firearms and get a pass. While Americans enjoy the right to keep and bear arms, this right is not there to be abused. One cannot deliberately intimidate others with their firearm nor can they recklessly discharge guns for any reason, or no reason at all. There are penalties for stupidity with firearms, especially if some harm comes to another person or someone's property is damaged.

The first word in this chapter was responsibility. It should be considered the first and last word in gun ownership. Exercising the right to bear arms does not endow anyone other than a commissioned peace officer with the authority to intervene in situations that may be none of their business. The armed citizen must, above all, exercise discretion and self-control.

When he wrote about the passage of "constitutional carry" laws in Kansas and West Virginia (the latter state's governor vetoed the bill), Bob Owens at Bearing Arms.com cautioned against "obnoxious and intentionally provocative" behavior to promote the cause. As noted earlier in this chapter, this sort of behavior can backfire, and some of the leading voices for gun rights and firearms ownership encourage people to exercise some restraint. "Tactics matter," Owens counseled. "Fight smart. Win."

Many people contend that there is nothing to fight about because the Second Amendment and various state constitutional right-to-bear-arms amendments are clear. That would be the "ideal world" situation, but this is the real world, and as we have seen, there are powerful and well-financed enemies of the Second Amendment working around the clock to erode it and turn the right to keep and bear arms into a privilege tightly regulated by an unsympathetic government.

Owens expressed confidence that "we will prevail… as long as some of the more 'politically challenged' on our side don't get in our way."

It is not enough to simply post chest-thumping messages on some gun rights Internet forum under a pseudonym, or to show up in a crowd at some rights rally. To protect this right to keep and bear arms, it is incumbent to become politically active and savvy. Network with other people, be alert to legislative proposals that may chip away at your rights, and be willing to discourage "rude behavior" within your own ranks.

Likewise, learn how to counter arguments from the gun prohibition lobby in a non-combative manner. Endeavor to be the reasonable and rational side of an argument that may find its way to YouTube or other social media, or the 5 o'clock news. Let the other side do the screaming and name-calling. Be zealous, not over-zealous.

The right to *bear* arms, by any rational definition, translates to being able to *carry* arms for all kinds of reasons, especially personal protection. If you write letters to the editor, are interviewed on the subject by a reporter, or engage in a dialogue with your elected representative, remind them that "bearing" arms means "carrying" arms, and that this civil right is not confined to one's home or place of business. Otherwise, it is not a right at all.

Carry with confidence, do it responsibly and work toward restoring political ground that has been lost over the years. Use it, don't abuse it, and you will never lose it.